GREAT AUTHORS OF
CLASSIC LITERATURE

Essential Authors for Children & Teens

GREAT AUTHORS OF

CLASSIC LITERATURE

EDITED BY JEANNE NAGLE

Britannica Educational Publishing
IN ASSOCIATION WITH
ROSEN
EDUCATIONAL SERVICES

Published in 2014 by Britannica Educational Publishing (a trademark of Encyclopædia Britannica, Inc.) in association with The Rosen Publishing Group, Inc.
29 East 21st Street, New York, NY 10010

Distributed exclusively by Rosen Publishing.
To see additional Britannica Educational Publishing titles, go to rosenpublishing.com

First Edition

Britannica Educational Publishing
J.E. Luebering: Director, Core Reference Group
Anthony L. Green: Editor, Compton's by Britannica

Rosen Publishing
Hope Lourie Killcoyne: Executive Editor
Jeanne Nagle: Senior Editor
Nelson Sá: Art Director
Brian Garvey: Designer
Cindy Reiman: Photography Manager
Introduction by Joseph Kampff

Cataloging-in-Publication Data

Great authors of classic literature/[editor] Jeanne Nagle.—First Edition.
pages cm.—(Essential Authors for Children & Teens)
Includes bibliographical references and index.
ISBN 978-1-62275-084-9 (library bound)
1. Authors—Biography—Juvenile literature. 2. Literature—History and criticism—Juvenile literature.
I. Nagle, Jeanne, editor of compilation.
PN451.G74 2014
809'.003—dc23
[B]

2013029273

Manufactured in the United States of America

On the cover, p. 3: *(top, left to right)* are Mark Twain, F. Scott Fitzgerald, and Jane Austen—three well-known authors of classic literature. *Time & Life Pictures/Getty Images, American Stock/Archive Photos/Getty Images, Stock Montage/Archive Photos/Getty Images*

Cover, p. 3 Ermolaev Alexander/Shutterstock.com; interior pages (books) © iStockphoto.com/AnthiaCumming, (typewriter keys) © iStockphoto.com/Marek Walica

Contents

14

44

65

94

101

121

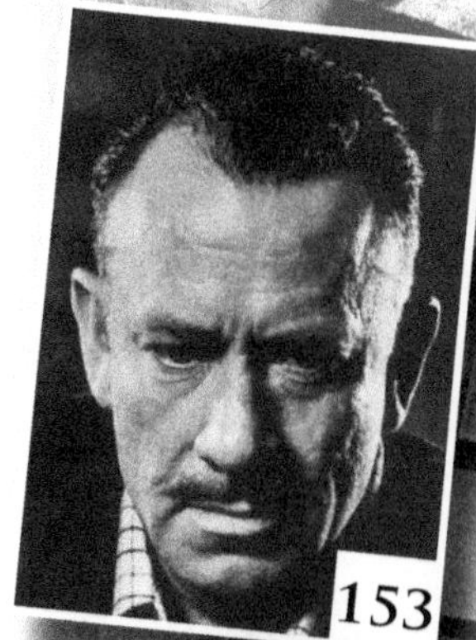
153

174

Illustration of Gulliver among the Lilliputians from a 19th-century edition of Jonathan Swift's Gulliver's Travels. Apic/Hulton Archive/Getty Images

Introduction

Classic literature can be off-putting to many people. The works of great authors such as Charles Dickens, Fyodor Dostoyevsky, and William Faulkner may seem outdated and inaccessible to casual readers who think *Great Expectations*, *Crime and Punishment*, and *The Sound and the Fury* are books one is forced to struggle through in high school or college. Yet far from being outdated, classic literature is timeless. Not only have many generations of readers been able to relate to classic literature, but they have also enjoyed it. *Great Authors of Classic Literature* is an excellent resource for people who have read works of classic literature, enjoyed them, and want to know more about the authors who created them.

Indeed, the lives of authors are often as compelling as their works. Knowing the story behind an author's motivation for writing, as well as the personal beliefs that have influenced the works, may even inspire someone who prefers popular novels to read the classics. For instance, readers interested in the history of feminism may be encouraged to read Virginia Woolf's challenging novels *Mrs. Dalloway*, *To the Lighthouse*, and *The Waves* when they learn she also wrote

one of the major texts of early feminism, *A Room of One's Own*.

Likewise, a connection with real-life historic events or controversy can pique reader interest in classic texts. Accused of producing and promoting obscene materials, authors James Joyce, Henry Miller, and Vladimir Nabokov saw their books—*Ulysses*, *Tropic of Cancer*, and *Lolita*, respectively—banned when they first appeared in print. D.H. Lawrence saw printing of several of his novels, including *Lady Chatterley's Lover*, stopped because of "indecent" content. These books, which are now considered classics, are still relevant to discussions regarding freedom of speech and censorship. Time spent in Europe gave African American novelist James Baldwin the critical distance to think and write incisively about racial issues in American society. Baldwin's novel *Another Country*, which deals explicitly with race and sexuality, is an important document of the civil rights movement in the United States.

Some of the stories by the authors in this volume have experienced a resurgence of sorts through different media. F. Scott Fitzgerald's *The Great Gatsby* has been made accessible to another generation of young-adult readers courtesy of a recent film adaptation starring Leonardo DiCaprio. The novel, which captures the riotous spirit of the Jazz Age as well as Fitzgerald's disillusionment with it, remains fresh today. Likewise, fans of the Broadway musical and film versions of *Les Misérables* may consider tackling Victor Hugo's immense novel to get the rest of this fascinating and moving story. Several film incarnations of works by Jane Austen have proved popular at the box office over the years. Many high schools in North America have chapters of the Jane Austen Society, which is dedicated to reading and enjoying her novels.

With biographies of more than 60 authors, *Great Authors of Classic Literature* is an excellent introduction to the writers whose stories have fascinated readers for generations and who remain popular and relevant today.

SHERWOOD ANDERSON

(b. 1876–d. 1941)

In his short stories and novels, the American writer Sherwood Anderson protested against the frustrations of ordinary people and against what he believed to be the narrow-minded conventions of his time. He was a master of colloquial speech. His concern with the unfulfilled lives of "little people" probably came from his early observations of life.

Sherwood Anderson was born in Camden, Ohio, on Sept. 13, 1876, the third child of eight. His father was an irresponsible man who could not hold a job long, but he was a colorful talker and storyteller. Most of Anderson's boyhood was spent in the small town of Clyde, Ohio, where he attended school irregularly.

When he was only 14, his mother died, and Anderson ended his formal education. The young man drifted from one job to another, finally welcoming the chance to serve in the Spanish-American War. When the war was over, he returned to Ohio

American author Sherwood Anderson, who is most noted for his classic short-story collection, Winesburg, Ohio. Eric Schaal/Time & Life Pictures/Getty Images

and eventually became manager of a paint factory in Elyria. It was at this time that Anderson began to write. He became more and more absorbed in writing. One day he walked out of the factory, apparently on a sudden impulse, never to return.

Sherwood joined his brother Karl, a magazine illustrator, in Chicago and took a job with an advertising agency. He became acquainted with the "Chicago group" of writers, which included Theodore Dreiser, Carl Sandburg, Ben Hecht, and Floyd Dell. Dreiser and Dell helped get Anderson's first novel, *Windy McPherson's Son*, published in 1916. It was a story of factory life, based on his own experiences.

His next books were *Marching Men* (1917), a novel about mines, and *Mid-American Chants* (1918), a book of poetry. Anderson was best as a short-story writer, and his most successful book was *Winesburg, Ohio*, published in 1919. The book is made up of short stories about small-town people.

After going abroad in 1921, Anderson returned to live in New Orleans and, later, New York. He finally settled in Marion, Va., where he edited two newspapers and continued to write. His autobiographical books are *A Story Teller's Story* (1924), *Tar: A Midwest Childhood* (1926), and *Sherwood Anderson's Memoirs* (1942). Anderson was married four times. He died in Colón, Pan., on March 8, 1941.

JANE AUSTEN

(b. 1775–d. 1817)

Through her portrayals of ordinary people in everyday life Jane Austen gave the genre of the novel its modern character. She began writing at an early age. At 15 she was writing plays and sketches for the amusement of her family, and by the time she was 21 she had begun to write novels that are among the finest in English literature.

Jane Austen was born on Dec. 16, 1775, in the parsonage of Steventon, a village in Hampshire, Eng. She had six brothers and one sister. Her father, the Reverend George Austen, was a rector of the village. Although she and her sister briefly attended several different schools, Jane was educated mainly by her father, who taught his own children and several pupils who boarded with the family. Her father retired when Jane was 25. By that time her brothers, two of whom later became admirals, had careers and families of their own. Jane, her sister Cassandra, and their parents went to live in Bath. After their father's death in 1805, the family lived temporarily in Southampton before finally settling in Chawton.

All Jane Austen's novels are love stories. However, neither Jane nor her sister ever married. There are hints of two or three romances in Jane's life, but little is known about them, for Cassandra destroyed all letters of a personal nature after Jane's death. The brothers had large families, and Jane was a favorite with her nephews and nieces.

Austen wrote two novels before she was 22. These she later revised and published as *Sense and Sensibility* (1811) and *Pride and Prejudice* (1813). She completed her third novel, *Northanger Abbey*, when she was 27 or 28, but it did not appear in print until after her death. She wrote three more novels in her late 30s: *Mansfield Park* (1814), *Emma* (1816), and *Persuasion* (published together with *Northanger Abbey* in 1818).

Austen wrote of the world she knew. Her novels portray the lives of the gentry and clergy of rural England, and they take place in the country villages and neighborhoods, with an occasional visit to Bath and London. Her world was small, but she saw it clearly and portrayed it with wit and detachment. She described her writing as "the little bit (two inches wide) of ivory on which I work with so fine a brush, as produces little effect after much labor."

Austen spent the last weeks of her life in Winchester, to be near her physician. She died on July 18, 1817, after a long illness and is buried in the cathedral at Winchester.

JAMES BALDWIN

(b. 1924–d. 1987)

An American novelist, essayist, and playwright, James Baldwin wrote with eloquence and passion on the subject of race in America. His main message was that blacks deserve to be treated like humans and that the civil rights problem derives from the insecurity of the white man, who needs a "Negro" to whom he can feel superior.

James Arthur Baldwin was born on Aug. 2, 1924, in the Harlem section of New York

City, to David and Berdis Jones Baldwin. His father, a Sunday minister, was very strict with his nine children, of whom James was the oldest. Teachers remembered James as a slight, intelligent, sad-looking boy. After graduating from high school in 1942, he worked at various jobs. A literary fellowship in 1948 enabled him to go to Europe, where he lived mostly in France. (In later years, from 1969, he became a self-styled "transatlantic commuter," living alternatively in the south of France and in New York and New England.) *Go Tell It on the Mountain* (1953), an autobiographical novel, helped establish him as a writer.

After his return to the United States in 1957, Baldwin became deeply involved in the civil rights movement. His book of essays, *Nobody Knows My Name* (1961), explores black–white relations in the United States. This theme also was central to his novel *Another Country* (1962), which examines sexual as well as racial issues. The *New Yorker* magazine gave over almost all of its Nov. 17, 1962, issue to a long article by Baldwin on the Black Muslim separatist movement and other aspects of the civil rights struggle. The article became a best seller in book form as *The Fire Next Time* (1963).

James Baldwin, posing for a portrait in France. Ulf Andersen/Getty Images

His play about racist oppression, *Blues for Mister Charlie*, played on Broadway to mixed reviews in 1964.

Baldwin continued to write until his death, publishing the short-story collection *Going to Meet the Man* (1965); the novels *Tell Me How Long the Train's Been Gone* (1968), *If Beale Street Could Talk* (1974), and *Just Above My Head* (1979); and *The Price of the Ticket* (1985), a collection of autobiographical writings. He died in St-Paul de Vence, France, on Nov. 30, 1987.

HONORÉ DE BALZAC

(b. 1799–d. 1850)

The great French novelist Honoré de Balzac wrote of life in France during his own time. His series of almost 80 novels and tales, which he called *La Comédie humaine* (*The Human Comedy*), forms a social history of France in the first half of the 1800s. In the works Balzac depicts more than 2,000 named characters, many of whom appear in later stories. The author labored mightily on each book. Writing the manuscript was only the first step. He would revise the printer's proof until little was left of the original text.

Balzac was born in Tours, France, on May 20, 1799. His father, a peasant's son, had become a banker and a supplier to Napoleon's army. His mother came from a middle-class family. In infancy he lived at his nurse's home. When he was 4 he was boarded out with strangers, coming home only on Sundays. When he was 7 he was sent to boarding school at Vendôme. He was a poor student, neglected by his parents and misunderstood by his teachers. He attended the University of Paris for a time, then was apprenticed to a notary. When he was 20 Balzac asserted himself. He begged his parents to support him for two years while he prepared to be a writer.

For eight years Balzac did not write under his own name. He earned much money but lost most of it in rash business ventures. In 1829 he wrote *Les Chouans*, the first volume of *The Human Comedy*. He spent more recklessly on houses, furniture, decorations, and new business ventures. He worked even harder to support this magnificent lifestyle.

Balzac's chief works are *La Peau de chagrin* (*The Wild Ass's Skin*, 1831), *Le Curé de Tours* (*The Vicar of Tours*, 1832), *Eugénie Grandet* (1833), *Le Lys dans la vallée* (*The Lily of the Valley*, 1836), *Le Père Goriot* (1835), *César Birotteau* (1837), *Ursule Mirouët* (1841), *Le Cousin Pons* (*Cousin Pons*, 1847), and *La Cousine Bette* (*Cousin Bette*, 1847).

In 1832 a Polish noblewoman, Eveline Hanska, wrote him a letter praising his work. They met the next year, and Balzac fell in love with her. They continued to meet and to correspond for several years. Her husband died in 1841, but she put off marrying Balzac until 1850. On Aug. 18, 1850, five months after their marriage, Balzac died in Paris.

THE BRONTË SISTERS, CHARLOTTE AND EMILY

Charlotte (b. 1816–d. 1855)
Emily (b. 1818–d. 1848)

The bleak, lonely moors of Yorkshire in England were the setting for two

great novels of the 19th century. These were Charlotte Brontë's *Jane Eyre* and Emily Brontë's *Wuthering Heights*. Readers today are still enthralled by their tragic, romantic stories and by the sense of brooding mystery that shrouds the tales. The youngest sister, Anne, was also a talented novelist, and her books have the same haunting quality.

Their father was Patrick Brontë, a Church of England priest. Irish-born, he had changed his name from the more commonplace Brunty. After serving in several parishes he moved with his wife, Maria Branwell Brontë, and their six small children to Haworth in Yorkshire in 1820. Soon after, Mrs. Brontë and the two eldest children died, leaving the father to care for the remaining three girls and a boy.

Charlotte, the eldest, was born in 1816. Emily was born in 1818 and Anne in 1820. Their brother Branwell was born in 1817. Left to themselves, the children wrote and told stories and walked over the desolate moors. They grew up largely self-educated. Branwell showed some talent for drawing. The girls determined to earn money for his art education. They took positions as

Portrait of (left to right) *Anne, Emily, and Charlotte Brontë, painted by their brother, Branwell.* DEA Picture Library/De Agostini/Getty Images

teachers and governesses (live-in teachers and caretakers), but they were unhappy at being separated and away from Haworth.

To keep the family together, Charlotte planned to start a school for girls at Haworth. She and Emily went to Brussels to learn foreign languages and school management. In 1844, using a small inheritance from an aunt, they prepared to open classes. Although they advertised, they received no pupils.

The failure of their venture left all the children at home. Seeking a way to help the family, Charlotte convinced Emily to publish a joint book of poems with her and Anne. In 1846 the girls brought out at their own expense *Poems by Currer, Ellis, and Acton Bell*. They chose masculine pen names but retained their own initials. Although critics liked the poems, only two volumes were sold.

As children they had all written many stories. Charlotte, as a young girl, alone filled 22 volumes, each with 60 to 100 pages of minute handwriting. Again they turned to writing as a source of income. By 1847, Charlotte had written *The Professor*; Emily, *Wuthering Heights*; and Anne, *Agnes*

Grey. After much difficulty Anne and Emily found a publisher, but Charlotte's book was not wanted. (It was not published until 1859.) However, one publisher expressed an interest in seeing more of her work. *Jane Eyre* was already started, and she hurriedly finished it. It was accepted at once; thus each of the sisters had a book published in 1847.

Jane Eyre was immediately successful; the other two did not fare so well. Critics were hostile to *Wuthering Heights*. They said it was too wild, too animal-like. But silent, reserved Emily had put all her deep feelings into the book, and gradually it came to be considered one of the finest novels in the English language. Emily lived only a short while after the publication of her book; she died of tuberculosis on Dec. 19, 1848, in Haworth. Anne died in 1849, also a victim of tuberculosis.

Charlotte published *Shirley* in 1849 and *Villette* in 1853. She was acclaimed by London literary society, especially by William Makepeace Thackeray. In 1854 she married her father's curate, Arthur Bell Nicholls. But only a year later, on March 31, 1855, she died of tuberculosis as her sisters had.

JOHN BUNYAN

(b. 1628–d. 1688)

After John Milton, the greatest literary genius produced by the Puritan movement in England was John Bunyan. His book *The Pilgrim's Progress* has been one of the most widely read and translated works in Western literature.

Bunyan was born in Elstow, Eng., in November 1628. As an adult, he joined a little congregation of Nonconformists and before long was preaching in the villages around Bedford with such great fervor and eloquence that people flocked to hear him. In 1660, he was arrested for disobeying the laws prohibiting Nonconformist meetings and was thrown into the jail in Bedford. There he remained for 12 years, with brief intervals of liberty. In 1672, King Charles suspended the laws against religious dissenters, and Bunyan was released, only to be imprisoned again three years later for illegal preaching.

It was probably during his second imprisonment that he wrote the first part of *The Pilgrim's Progress*. The novel tells the story of how Christian, the hero, flees from the City of Destruction and starts on a pilgrimage, during which he faces many perils. Because he could create realistic characters and because he told stories with dramatic vigor, Bunyan paved the way for a new kind of literature—the novel. Some critics, indeed, consider him the father of the English novel.

Of Bunyan's more than 60 published works, the best known are *Grace Abounding to the Chief of Sinners* (1666), *The Pilgrim's Progress* (Part I, 1678; Part II, 1684), *The Life and Death of Mr. Badman* (1680), and *The Holy War for Mansoul* (1682).

In the last years of his life Bunyan won increasing fame both as a preacher and as a writer. On a journey to preach in London, he was caught in a drenching rain. A violent fever seized him, and he died in London on Aug. 31, 1688.

SAMUEL BUTLER

(b. 1835–d. 1902)

English author Samuel Butler was a musician and painter in Victorian

England. Yet it is for his novels that he is best remembered.

Butler was born in Nottinghamshire, Eng., on Dec. 4, 1835, the son of a clergyman. He graduated from St. John's College,

English author Samuel Butler. Hulton Archive/Getty Images

Cambridge, in 1858. A religious argument with his father led him to move to New Zealand in 1859. In 1864 he returned to England to settle for the rest of his life in London.

Butler's writings portray his personal attempt to come to terms with religion, the Industrial Revolution, the theory of evolution, and the social atmosphere of his time. In his lifetime he was acclaimed for the novel *Erewhon* (1872), a satirical look at the age in which he lived. (The title is roughly "nowhere" spelled backward.) *The Way of All Flesh*, published the year after his death, is regarded as his masterpiece. It is an autobiographical condemnation of Victorian morality. Butler died in London on June 18, 1902.

WILLA CATHER

(b. 1873–d. 1947)

In such classic American novels as *O Pioneers!* Willa Cather wrote of people she had known as a girl in Nebraska. Her friends were native Americans as well as European immigrants and their children.

She showed how these pioneers were able to adapt to the rugged prairie life in the western area of America. For her depictions of this valiant spirit, Willa Cather won wide acclaim as a novelist.

Willa Sibert Cather was born on Dec. 7, 1873, on a farm near the town of Winchester, Va. The Cather family had been living in Virginia for four generations. When Cather was 9 years old, her father bought a ranch that was located near Red Cloud, Neb. The child was excited by the change from a settled, eastern community to a semifrontier area where she was free to roam outdoors. Often she would ride her pony to a neighbor's farm and listen to old immigrant women tell stories of their childhood experiences and adventures in Sweden or Bohemia.

There were no schools near the ranch, so she studied at home. A neighbor taught her Latin, and Cather read English classics aloud to her grandmother. When Cather was in her teens the family moved into the village. She attended Red Cloud High School and the University of Nebraska. After graduation in 1895 she worked on a Pittsburgh newspaper for six years and then taught high school for a time. On vacations she traveled to Europe and the American Southwest.

Meanwhile, she contributed stories to *McClure's Magazine*. She also accepted a post on the magazine, and in 1908 she became its managing editor. But editing left her little time for creative writing, and in 1912 she resigned to devote full time to writing her own stories.

Her first novel was unsuccessful, but when she turned to frontier themes she won a wide audience. *O Pioneers!*, published in 1913, was followed by *Song of the Lark* (1915) and *My Ántonia* (1918). *One of Ours* (1922), which won the Pulitzer Prize, and *A Lost Lady* (1923) mourned the passing of the pioneer spirit in the Middle West. Also popular were *Death Comes for the Archbishop* (1927), a study of Roman Catholic missionaries in New Mexico, and *Shadows on the Rock* (1931), a story of early Quebec. She described her clean, meticulous writing style as "*démeuble*" (unfurnished).

Cather never married. She lived quietly in New York City and traveled frequently in Europe, avoiding public appearances whenever possible. She remained loyal to childhood friends and visited them often. She died in New York City on April 24, 1947.

MIGUEL DE CERVANTES

(b. 1547–d. 1616)

Some 400 years ago Miguel de Cervantes wrote a book that made him the most important figure in Spanish literature to this day. Six editions of *Don Quixote* were printed in the first year after the publication of the first part (1605). Translations into foreign languages were begun almost immediately. It is one of the most popular books ever written.

Cervantes was born in the town of Alcalá de Henares, near Madrid, in the autumn of 1547. His father, Rodrigo de Cervantes, was a poor and obscure surgeon. There is no evidence that Miguel attended the university of his native town or of any other of the towns in which he spent his youth—Valladolid, Seville, and Madrid.

By the end of 1569, when he was 22, Cervantes was in Rome, where he served as a gentleman-in-waiting in the household of Cardinal Acquaviva. The next year he enlisted in the Spanish militia, then on duty in Italy. In October 1571 he took part in the battle of

Lepanto, a famous sea fight in which the allied fleets of Spain and the Italian cities destroyed the Turkish fleet. In this battle Cervantes suffered three gunshot wounds, one of which permanently crippled his left hand.

Four years later the ship on which Cervantes was returning to Spain was captured by Barbary pirates. He and his brother were carried as slaves to Algiers. Although his brother was able to earn his freedom relatively quickly, Miguel was held for several more years. He made several unsuccessful attempts to escape and partly as a result of those attempts became known for his bravery and leadership among the community of captives.

After five years of slavery, Cervantes was at last ransomed by his relatives and friends and returned to Spain. With a maimed hand, he could not continue soldiering, and the king turned a deaf ear to his requests for an appointment; so he tried writing. In the next few years he turned out 20 or 30 plays as well as a pastoral romance, *Galatea*. But they were all failures, more or less. This convinced Cervantes that he could never earn his bread by his pen.

For a few months in 1597–98 Cervantes was imprisoned because he could not make up for a shortage in his accounts as tax collector, caused by the failure of the banker to whom he had entrusted the money. He may have conceived of the idea for *Don Quixote* while he was in prison. Apparently he was jailed again in about 1603, but nothing certain is known about these years. In 1604 he came to Valladolid with the manuscript of the first part of his most famous tale.

Don Quixote is the story of an elderly gentleman of La Mancha, the bare and monotonous plateau of central Spain. He reads so many of the exaggerated romances of chivalry of his day that he finally believes them to be true. One day he sets forth himself as a knight-errant on his old horse, Rosinante. A shrewd, good-natured peasant of his village, Sancho Panza, goes with him as his squire. Don Quixote's overly romantic view of the world contrasts with the realistic and practical view of Sancho Panza as they experience a series of comic adventures. The influence of the book was so great, even in translation, that the word "quixotic," meaning "foolishly impractical" or "idealistic," became part of the English language.

In addition to *Don Quixote* Cervantes published several other popular works.

Statue of Miguel de Cervantes, erected in his hometown of Valladolid, Spain. Hemera/Thinkstock

These included a collection of short fiction entitled *Novelas ejemplares* (1613; *Exemplary Novels*) and his last romance, *Los trabaios de Persiles y Sigismunda, historia setentrional* (*The Labors of Persiles and Sigismunda: A Northern Story*), which was published posthumously in 1617.

It is through *Don Quixote*, however, that Cervantes made his greatest and most lasting contribution to literature. The first part of the book was published in 1605, when Cervantes was 57. Despite its huge success, he received little money because he sold his rights in the book to his publisher. While the fame of *Don Quixote* spread through Europe, Cervantes lived in poverty, dependent upon rich patrons. He published the second part of *Don Quixote* in 1615. Cervantes died on April 22, 1616, in Madrid.

KATE CHOPIN

(b. 1851–d. 1904)

With tales of passionate, disconnected women trying to free themselves from the constraints of society, Kate Chopin became one of the late

19th century's best-known and most controversial writers. Interest in Chopin was rekindled in the late 20th century because her work foreshadowed that era's feminist literary themes.

Katherine O'Flaherty was born on Feb. 8, 1851, in St. Louis, Mo., into a fairly wealthy family. Her father, an Irish immigrant, had moved from place to place until making his fortune as a businessman and settling in St. Louis. A curious and imaginative child, Kate was schooled in the Sacred Heart Academy convent school. She developed a love for the freedom of the outdoors, and her natural inquisitiveness and exploratory nature often got her into trouble, usually because she had somehow behaved in a manner that was considered inappropriate for a young girl.

In 1870, at the age of just 20, she married Oscar Chopin, a cotton trader from Louisiana. Her family, Southern sympathizers during the American Civil War, approved of the arrangement, and she moved to New Orleans with her new husband. The couple's first child was born a little over a year later on Dec. 10, 1871. The family remained in New Orleans until they relocated to Cloutierville near Natchitoches

Parish, La., shortly after their sixth and last child was born in 1879.

In December of 1882 Oscar Chopin died of malaria. He was nearly bankrupt at the time of his passing and left his family in dire financial straits. Kate moved back to St. Louis in 1884 and began a new phase of her life as a writer. Her writing career spanned about 14 years and included over 100 novels, stories, poems, reviews, plays, and essays.

Chopin's first novel, *At Fault* (1890), was undistinguished, but her reputation grew when her short fiction about Creole and Cajun life in Louisiana began appearing in magazines in 1889. The finely crafted stories were collected in *Bayou Folk* (1894) and *A Night in Acadie* (1897); the latter in particular was condemned by some critics for its unabashed treatment of sensuality.

In 1897, she began what many consider her finest work, *The Awakening*, which focused on a woman trapped in a conventional marriage that denied her the creative outlets and love she craved. The novel, published in 1899, stirred a storm of outrage among shocked critics for its frank depiction of the protagonist's sexual and artistic awakening. Nearly ignored for 50 years, *The Awakening* was rediscovered during the

1960s and made Chopin a standard-bearer of the women's rights movement. Her masterpiece also garnered acclaim for its writing and modern sensibility during its critical reevaluation.

On Aug. 20, 1904, Chopin suffered a cerebral hemorrhage after attending the world's fair in St. Louis. She died there two days later.

JOSEPH CONRAD

(b. 1857–d. 1924)

At the age of 20, Polish-born Joseph Conrad could speak no English; yet in his lifetime he would write outstanding novels and stories in that language. His tales of seafaring life depicted the concerns of all people: hazards in nature, the need for loyalty, and the danger in greed.

He was born Jósef Teodor Konrad Korzeniowski to a Polish family on Dec. 3, 1857, in what is now Ukraine. He was orphaned in 1869 and was brought up by his uncle, who hoped that he would become a lawyer. But Conrad wanted to be a sailor. In October 1874 he moved to Marseilles,

France, and went to sea at age 17. In July 1876 he sailed as steward on the *St-Antoine*. It is likely that he took part in the smuggling of weapons, as later described in his novel *Nostromo*. It is known that in 1878 he was recovering from a mysterious chest wound that his uncle claimed was self-inflicted. Conrad, however, encouraged people to think he had suffered the injury in a duel.

In April 1878 he was sufficiently recovered to be a deckhand on the British freighter *Mavis*, and for the next 16 years he served in the British merchant navy. In 1886 he became eligible to be a ship's captain and also received British citizenship. His sea travels often took him to the Far East, and his experiences provided him with material for the novels and stories he would later write.

Back in London in 1889, he began his first novel, *Almayer's Folly*, but interrupted this work to visit Africa—a dream he had had since childhood. He commanded a steamboat on the Congo River, and, though he became very ill for awhile, the adventure provided him with the seed of his most famous story, the novella *Heart of Darkness*, published in 1899.

Under his anglicized name of Joseph Conrad, he published *Almayer's Folly* in April 1895. It did not sell well but got critical praise. However, he was soon to write his finest novels—*Lord Jim* (1900), *Nostromo* (1904), *Secret Agent* (1907), and *Under Western Eyes* (1911). In 1919 he settled in Bishopsbourne, Eng., where he died on Aug. 3, 1924.

JAMES FENIMORE COOPER

(b. 1789–d. 1851)

The first American novelist to achieve worldwide fame was James Fenimore Cooper. His stories were translated into foreign languages as soon as they were published. Robert Louis Stevenson called him "Cooper of the wood and wave," because he wrote about American Indians and pioneers in the forest and sailors on the high seas.

Cooper was born in Burlington, N.J., on Sept. 15, 1789. When he was a year old the family moved to a large estate on Otsego Lake, N.Y. There his father, William Cooper, laid

Portrait of author James Fenimore Cooper, by John Wesley Jarvis. DEA Picture Library/De Agostini/Getty Images

out Cooperstown. The region was still a wilderness. Indians came to trade at the village.

In 1803 Cooper went to Yale. He neglected his studies to spend most of his time outdoors and was expelled after three years. He went to sea for five years, first as a merchant sailor, then as a midshipman in the Navy. In 1811 he married and went to live at his wife's home in Westchester County, N.Y. In 1833, after spending years traveling abroad, he settled on his estate in Cooperstown. He died there on Sept. 14, 1851.

Cooper's first novel, *Precaution*, was published in 1820. A story of English society life, it was a complete failure. The next year he turned to the American scene and won instant popularity with a Revolutionary War novel, *The Spy*. In 1823 Cooper wrote *The Pioneers*, the first of five Leatherstocking Tales. The intrepid scout Leatherstocking (sometimes called Natty Bumppo or Hawkeye) figures in all these stories. Cooper described him as "a philosopher of the wilderness, simple-minded, faithful, utterly without fear, and yet prudent." With *The Last of the Mohicans* Cooper reached the height of his fame. The "last Mohican" is the noble Uncas. Cooper's style was rather careless but swift moving.

The novels in the Leatherstocking series should be read in this order: *The Deerslayer* (1841), *The Pathfinder* (1840), *The Last of the Mohicans* (1826), *The Pioneers* (1823), and *The Prairie* (1827). The most popular of his sea stories are *The Pilot* (1823) and *The Red Rover* (1828).

STEPHEN CRANE

(b. 1871–d. 1900)

A novelist, poet, and short-story writer, Stephen Crane is considered one of the most outstanding American novelists and short-story writers of the 19th century. He is regarded as a pioneer of social and psychological realism in American literature.

Crane was born in Newark, N.J., on Nov. 1, 1871, into a family in which there were many Methodist ministers. He rebelled in many ways against the family's morality, but his writings were to reflect his religious background. His schooling was sporadic; nonetheless, he read all the 19th-century English writers and the Greek and Latin classics.

Crane worked as a freelance writer in New York City in the early 1890s, and there he wrote *Maggie: A Girl of the Streets*, first published in 1893. The novel, about an abused slum girl's descent into prostitution and her eventual suicide, displayed a realism that set the literary trend of the following generation. He then wrote *Red Badge of Courage* (1895), which he intended to be "a psychological portrayal of fear." Crane also achieved mastery of the short story. His volumes of them include *The Little Regiment, and Other Episodes of the American Civil War* (1896) and *The Open Boat, and Other Tales of Adventure* (1898).

Crane's poetry was of a rhymeless, rhythmic, free-form style. He also did journalistic reporting in Greece and Cuba. Crane died on June 5, 1900, in Badenweiler, Ger., of tuberculosis, compounded by a recurring malarial fever he had contracted in Cuba while reporting on the Spanish-American War.

DANIEL DEFOE

(b. 1660–d. 1731)

Daniel Defoe was a man of many talents, among them businessman and pamphleteer. He is perhaps best known, however, as the author of *Robinson Crusoe* and *Moll Flanders*.

Defoe was born in London in 1660. His father, James Foe, was a fairly prosperous chandler. The Foes were Dissenters, or Nonconformists, who did not believe in certain practices of the Church of England. At age 14 Daniel was sent to a Dissenters' academy. In addition to the traditional Latin and Greek, he studied French, Italian, Spanish, and history and became especially well educated in geography. He studied for the ministry but instead went into business. Engaged in financial speculation and foreign trade, he visited France and lived in Spain for a time. He began to use the name Defoe, which may have been the family's original Flemish name.

Meanwhile, he began writing about public affairs. In witty and often bold pamphlets, verse, and periodicals, he called for reforms and advances in religious practices, economics, social welfare, and politics. In his *Essay on Projects*, written in 1698, he suggested a national bank, reformed bankruptcy laws, asylums, and academies of learning. He stressed the need for tolerance, often using satire for emphasis. In *The True-Born Englishman* (1701), he assailed his country's prejudice against its foreign-born king.

In 1702 Defoe wrote a pamphlet titled *The Shortest-Way with the Dissenters*, satirizing the Tories' persecution of Dissenters. Infuriated, the government had him fined, locked in a pillory, and imprisoned in 1703. After some months in prison he was released through the influence of Robert Harley, a statesman who became his patron. Defoe then wrote political pamphlets for Harley and served as his secret agent in working for the union of Scotland and England.

In 1704 Defoe started and almost single-handedly wrote the *Review*. It was the first of many "essay periodicals"—forerunners of the modern newspaper—with which he was connected. He published it until 1713.

Late in life Defoe began yet another career, writing fiction. As a novelist, he was celebrated for his insight into human nature. His plain, direct style and an accumulation of concrete, realistic details make his stories seem true to life. His lifelong love of travel and adventure is reflected in his "true histories" of pirates and thieves, in which he spiced facts with imagination. In 1719 he published the novel *Robinson*

Crusoe, which was drawn partly from the memoirs of castaways, especially the Scottish sailor Alexander Selkirk. His other major works include two published in 1722: *Moll Flanders*, a novel that vividly recounts the urban struggles of its streetwise title character, and *A Journal of the Plague Year*, a fictionalized account of London's Great Plague of 1664–65.

Defoe published his final novel, *Roxana*, in 1724. He died in London on April 24, 1731.

CHARLES DICKENS

(b. 1812–d. 1870)

No English author of the 19th century was more popular than the novelist Charles Dickens. With a reporter's eye for the details of daily life, a fine ear for the subtleties of common speech, and unmatched powers of character creation, Dickens created a body of work that brought him worldwide fame.

Charles John Huffam Dickens was born on Feb. 7, 1812, in Portsmouth, Eng. He was the second of eight children. His father, John

Dickens, was a clerk in a navy office, a job that required him to move his family frequently. In 1817 the family settled in the town of Chatham, southeast of London, where Charles attended school and developed an interest in English novels of the 18th century.

John Dickens was a habitually poor manager of money. In 1824 he was sent with his family to the Marshalsea Prison for debt. Charles, the eldest son, did not go to prison, but he was pulled from school and put to work in a factory. A timely inheritance restored the family to something like comfortable means, and Charles had a few quiet years at a private school in London.

After finishing his schooling, Dickens became a clerk in a law office, then a reporter in the law courts and in the House of Commons. In 1834 he joined the staff of the *Morning Chronicle*, for which he traveled to other cities and towns to report election speeches. His first attempt at creative writing began with stories and descriptive essays he contributed to magazines and newspapers under the name of Boz, the family nickname of a younger brother. These were collected and in February 1836 reprinted as *Sketches by "Boz,"* which was well received.

That same month the publishers Chapman and Hall asked Dickens to write stories to accompany a monthly series of comic illustrations by a noted artist. Originally the stories and illustrations were to deal with a group of Londoners in a hunting and fishing club, but Dickens, knowing little of the subject, suggested changing the focus to travel. The publishers agreed, and Dickens went on to create Mr. Pickwick; within a few months *The Pickwick Papers* had made Dickens the most popular author of the day.

In 1836 Dickens resigned from his newspaper job and became editor of a new monthly magazine, *Bentley's Miscellany*, in which he serialized the novel *Oliver Twist* (1837–39). His other serialized novels of this period were *Nicholas Nickleby* (1838–39), *The Old Curiosity Shop* (1840–41), and the historical novel *Barnaby Rudge* (1841). In April 1836, Dickens married Catherine Hogarth, the daughter of a newspaper associate. The first of their 10 children was born in 1837.

Exhausted by his intense work schedule, Dickens set out for a five-month vacation in the United States in early 1842. Treated as a literary celebrity, he received an enthusiastic welcome. While in the United States,

Charles Dickens, posing for a photographic portrait in the 1850s. Rischgitz/Hulton Archive/Getty Images

Dickens spoke of the need for an international copyright agreement that would protect the rights of both American and British writers. He felt that it was unfair and unjust that American publishers could print and sell his books without permission from him and without paying him any royalties. He pointed out that all British authors were equally victimized; he also acknowledged that American authors, such as Edgar Allan Poe, suffered from the pirating of their works in England.

In time Dickens's rosy view of the United States faded. His disillusionment with the United States is revealed in his nonfiction book *American Notes* (1842) and in the novel *Martin Chuzzlewit* (1843–44).

The first of Dickens's popular Christmas stories, *A Christmas Carol*, was conceived and written in a few weeks in 1843. It became the most enduring Christmas myth of modern literature. Further Christmas books, essays, and stories followed annually (except in 1847) through 1867, but none equaled the *Carol* in quality.

Dickens's first novel to display his new maturity as a writer was *Dombey and Son* (1846–48). Although serialized, this novel was clearly a product of more thorough planning.

His next novel, *David Copperfield* (1849–50), shows the author at the height of his powers.

Despite his great success as a novelist, Dickens did not wish to limit himself to book writing. He attempted or planned several periodical ventures in the 1840s and 1850s. In 1846 he became editor of the newly founded liberal newspaper the *Daily News*, but within weeks he decided that he was not suited for the job and resigned. In 1850 he finally achieved journalistic success with *Household Words*, a weekly journal that he founded and edited. This publication and its successor, *All the Year Round*, were popular collections of fiction, poetry, and essays on a wide range of topics. Dickens contributed several serials of his own, including novels.

Dickens's novels of the 1850s were much darker than their predecessors. *Bleak House* (1852–53) and *Little Dorrit* (1855–57) attack the injustices of the English legal system, and *Hard Times* (1854) explores the dehumanizing effects of industrialization on workers and communities. The humor in these novels takes the form of harsh satire.

The dark tone of these novels reflected a decline in Dickens's spirits due to personal difficulties, including the disintegration of his marriage. Around the time of his

separation from his wife, Dickens began devoting much of his time to public readings from his novels. The early readings consisted entirely of Christmas books, but he soon added episodes from the novels and magazine Christmas stories. He made a number of successful tours in England, Scotland, and Ireland and in 1867-68 completed a successful tour in the United States.

Dickens greatly enjoyed his readings until, near the end, he was becoming ill and exhausted. He wrote much less in the 1860s, but he remained inventive. *A Tale of Two Cities* (1859), set during the French Revolution, was his first historical novel since *Barnaby Rudge*. It continues to be one of his most popular novels. *Great Expectations* (1860–61) proved a great critical and popular success. *Our Mutual Friend* (1864–65) continued his ongoing critique of wealth and class values.

Dickens gave his final public reading in London in March 1870. Thereafter he worked on his last novel, *The Mystery of Edwin Drood*, at Gad's Hill, his country house near his boyhood home in Chatham. Dickens died at home on June 9, 1870, leaving the book unfinished. He was buried in Westminster Abbey in London.

JOHN DOS PASSOS

(b. 1896–d. 1970)

U.S. author John Dos Passos was a social historian who championed the underdog. He was also the creator of a fresh and original technique in novel writing.

John Roderigo Dos Passos was born on Jan. 14, 1896, in Chicago, Ill. His father, also named John, was a lawyer who had been a drummer boy in the American Civil War. The Dos Passos family traveled in many countries, including England, where for a time John attended school. He entered Harvard University in 1912 with the vague intention of becoming an architect. He graduated in 1916, still with no definite ambition to be a writer.

Soon after graduation, Dos Passos went to Spain to study architecture. Early in 1917, during World War I, he joined the ambulance service of the Allies. When the United States entered the war, Dos Passos enlisted in the Medical Corps.

After the war he traveled widely, writing for newspapers and magazines. His wartime experience gave Dos Passos the inspiration and subject matter for his first novel, *One*

Man's Initiation—1917, published in England in 1920. In 1921 he published *Three Soldiers*, which was well received by both critics and the public. It is a violent protest against war.

Manhattan Transfer (1925) was a turning point in Dos Passos's writing career. In this novel he used several innovations in technique. One device is the telling of many separate stories simultaneously in a sort of impressionistic effort to capture the pace and atmosphere of big-city life.

Dos Passos became increasingly interested in social and political issues and more and more concerned with the problems of poor people. For a time he supported leftist causes. Later, however, he became disillusioned with communism as a method for social reform.

His most important works are *The 42nd Parallel* (1930), *Nineteen Nineteen* (1932), and *The Big Money* (1936), which make up the trilogy *U.S.A.* In these novels Dos Passos used some of the literary devices he had introduced in *Manhattan Transfer*. Intermingled with the stories are sketches of prominent people who were living during the period covered. He also used newspaper headlines and bits from popular songs to re-create the mood of the time.

Another trilogy, *District of Columbia*, was made up of *Adventures of a Young Man* (1939), *Number One* (1943), and *The Grand Design* (1949). His growing conservatism was evident in these works. He also published poems, essays, plays, and travel books. He was married twice and had one daughter. Dos Passos died in Baltimore, Md., on Sept. 29, 1970.

FYODOR DOSTOYEVSKY

(b. 1821–d. 1881)

The works of Russian novelist and short-story writer Fyodor Dostoyevsky had an immense influence on 20th-century fiction. His works are often called prophetic because he so accurately predicted how Russia's revolutionaries would behave if they came to power. In his time he was also renowned for his activity as a journalist.

Fyodor Mikhaylovich Dostoyevsky was born on Oct. 30, 1821, in Moscow. Unlike many other Russian writers of the first part of the 19th century, such as Leo Tolstoy and Ivan Turgenev, Dostoyevsky was not born into the landed gentry. His father, a retired military surgeon, served as a doctor at the Mariinsky Hospital for the Poor in Moscow, where he treated charity cases while also conducting a private practice. His mother was a cultured woman from a merchant family. In 1828 his father managed to earn the rank of a nobleman and bought an estate, where the family spent the summer months.

Until 1833 Dostoyevsky was educated at home, before being sent to a day school and then to a boarding school. Later he was a student in the Academy of Military Engineering in St. Petersburg, a career as a military engineer having been marked out for him by his father. As a child and as a student, Dostoyevsky was drawn to Romantic and Gothic fiction. Not long after completing his degree (1843) and becoming a sublieutenant, Dostoyevsky resigned his commission to commence a hazardous career as a writer living off his pen.

The first work Dostoyevsky published was a translation of Honoré de Balzac's novel *Eugénie Grandet*; he did not have to toil long in obscurity. No sooner had he written his first novella, *Bednyye lyudi* (1846; *Poor Folk*), than he was hailed as the great new talent of Russian literature by the most influential critic of his day, Vissarion Belinsky. In the next few years Dostoyevsky published a number of stories, including *Belyye nochi* ("White Nights"), which depicts the mentality of a dreamer, and a novella, *Dvoynik* (1846; *The Double*), a study in schizophrenia.

In 1849 Dostoyevsky was arrested along with members of a group devoted to revolution and illegal propaganda. He spent eight months in prison until, on December 22, the prisoners were led without warning to the Semyonovsky Square, where a sentence of death by firing squad was pronounced. Dostoyevsky was among the first three prisoners to be shot. At the last possible moment, the guns were lowered and a messenger arrived with the information that the tsar had deigned to spare their lives. Instead of being executed, Dostoyevsky was sentenced to four years in a Siberian prison labor camp, to be followed by an indefinite term as a soldier. After his return to Russia 10 years later, he wrote a novel based on his prison camp experiences, *Zapiski iz myortvogo doma* (1861–62; *The House of the Dead*).

Dostoyevsky is best known for his novella *Notes from the Underground* (1864) and for four long novels, *Crime and Punishment* (1866), *The Idiot* (1868–69), *The Possessed* (1872; also and more accurately known as *The Demons* and *The Devils*), and *The Brothers Karamazov* (1879–80). These major works are renowned as great "novels of ideas" that treat timeless and timely issues in philosophy and politics. These novels also broke new ground with their experiments in literary form.

In 1873 Dostoyevsky assumed the editorship of the conservative journal *Grazhdanin* ("The Citizen"), where he published an irregular column entitled *Dnevnik pisatelya* ("The Diary of a Writer"). A one-man journal, for which Dostoyevsky served as editor, publisher, and sole contributor, the *Diary* represented an attempt to initiate a new literary genre. Each monthly issue contained diverse kinds of material: short stories, plans for possible stories, autobiographical essays, sketches that seem to lie on the boundary between fiction and journalism, psychological analyses of sensational crimes, literary criticism, and political commentary. The *Diary* proved immensely popular and financially rewarding.

After finishing *The Brothers Karamazov,* Dostoyevsky resumed the monthly *Diary* but lived to publish only a single issue (January 1881) before dying of a hemorrhage on Jan. 28, 1881, in St. Petersburg.

THEODORE DREISER

(b. 1871–d. 1945)

Novelist Theodore Dreiser was a leading American figure in the literary movement known as naturalism, which aimed to portray life in a realistic manner and depicted people as victims of blind forces and their own uncontrolled passions. Dreiser's first novel, *Sister Carrie*, was so shocking for its time that the publisher almost refused to publish it. The book was eventually published, but only in an altered form. Many of Dreiser's other novels sparked a similar response.

Dreiser was born in Terre Haute, Ind., on Aug. 27, 1871. He was the 12th of 13 children in a poor family. His formal education was meager, but he finished a year at Indiana University before beginning a career in journalism that led him to New York City in 1894. Supported by his prosperous composer brother Paul (who spelled his name Dresser), he wrote magazine articles. Distressed over the hostile reception of his *Sister Carrie* (1900), he had a nervous breakdown. His next novel, *Jennie Gerhardt* (1911), was likewise condemned because, like *Sister Carrie*, it was a story of unconventional sexual relationships.

Dreiser's next two novels, *The Financier* (1912) and *The Titan* (1914), were based on the exploits of the American transportation magnate Charles Tyson Yerkes. When these books were also unsuccessful, Dreiser turned from the novel to other forms of writing for the next 10 years. The publication of *An American Tragedy* (1925), based on a famous murder case, was his greatest critical and financial success. After this novel the quality and quantity of his work fell sharply. His last two novels, *The Bulwark* (1946) and *The Stoic* (1947), were published after his death. Dreiser died in Hollywood, Calif., on Dec. 28, 1945.

GEORGE ELIOT

(b. 1819–d. 1880)

One of England's foremost novelists of the 19th century was Mary Ann (or Marian) Evans, who wrote under the pen name George Eliot. In such novels as *Silas*

Portrait of English author George Eliot, which was the pseudonym of Mary Ann (Marian) Evans. London Stereoscopic Company/Hulton Archive/Getty Images

Marner and *The Mill on the Floss*, Eliot created realistic pictures of English country life. *Middlemarch*, her masterpiece, skillfully depicts every class of society in a provincial town. Eliot wrote with a psychological depth that would become characteristic of modern fiction.

Mary Ann Evans was born in Warwickshire, Eng., on Nov. 22, 1819. She spent her first years on an estate where her father worked. At age 7 she was sent to boarding school, where she received a strongly Christian education. Mary Ann's mother died when the girl was 16. In 1841 Mary Ann moved with her father to nearby Coventry.

There Marian (as she began writing her name) became a close friend of Charles Bray and his family. Bray, a prosperous manufacturer, had forsaken conventional Christianity in favor of his own system of ethics. Bray's ideas greatly influenced the girl, much to her father's anguish. During these years she translated David Friedrich Strauss's *Life of Jesus Critically Examined* from the original German.

After her father's death in 1849, Marian lived with the Brays. In 1851 she took a job in London as assistant editor of the *Westminster Review*. She often worked 18 hours a day, but she still found time for social life with the leading writers and thinkers of the day. Among them was George Henry Lewes, a fairly well-known but not very successful journalist. Lewes's wife had deserted him, leaving him their three young sons. In 1854 Marian became his common-law wife in a union that lasted until his death.

Lewes soon recognized Marian's growing genius and urged her to try fiction. Her first effort was a short story, "The Sad Fortunes of the Reverend Amos Barton." It was accepted by *Blackwood's Magazine* for the January 1857 issue. Marian used her masculine pen name, which she chose to evade prejudice against women writers. For some years no one but Lewes knew who George Eliot was. *Blackwood's* accepted several more stories and reprinted them in a book, *Scenes of Clerical Life*, published in 1858.

For the next 20 years each new book by George Eliot was acclaimed by the critics and widely read by the public. She published *Adam Bede* in 1859; *The Mill on the Floss* (1860); *Silas Marner* (1861); *Romola* (1862–63); *Felix Holt the Radical* (1866); *The Spanish Gypsy* (1868), a dramatic poem; *Brother and Sister* (1869), a sonnet sequence; *Middlemarch* (1871–72); *Daniel Deronda* (1876);

and *Impressions of Theophrastus Such* (1879). Income from the books enabled George Eliot and Lewes to live fashionably, to entertain, and to travel.

The couple's happy life together ended with Lewes's death in 1878. George Eliot wrote no more, and for a long time she mourned him deeply. In 1880 she married John W. Cross. Only a few months later, on Dec. 22, 1880, she died. Cross arranged her letters and journals into a collection titled *Life* (1885). This work has been the main source for succeeding biographies.

RALPH ELLISON

(b. 1914–d. 1994)

For seven years Ralph Ellison poured both his firsthand awareness of the plight of African Americans and his belief in the United States as a land of possibility into the novel that became *Invisible Man*. On the basis of that single work, published in 1952, Ellison established his reputation as a major 20th-century American writer.

Ralph Waldo Ellison was born in Oklahoma City, Okla., on March 1, 1914.

He was named after Ralph Waldo Emerson, the 19th-century essayist, by his father, a construction worker and avid reader. As a boy he was interested in music and reading, and at age 8 he began to play the trumpet. Later he studied classical music at Tuskegee Institute (now University) in Alabama.

In 1936 Ellison visited New York City to study sculpture and to work with the Federal Writers' Project. There he met the African American authors Langston Hughes and Richard Wright, who inspired him to become a writer. In 1937 Ellison moved to New York City, and he was soon contributing essays, short stories, and articles to several publications.

After serving in World War II, Ellison wrote *Invisible Man*, which won the 1953 National Book Award for fiction. In a complex and symbolic narrative, the partly autobiographical novel relates one African American's struggle to find his place in a racially divided society while simultaneously exploring the universal human search for identity. Like the novel, many of Ellison's short stories explore the relationship of African Americans to their heritage and the place of blacks in white society. Ellison's other full-length works, *Shadow and Act*

(1964) and *Going to the Territory* (1986), were collections of essays and interviews.

Ellison lectured widely on African American culture, folklore, and creative writing and taught at several U.S. colleges and universities. After a fire destroyed much of the manuscript of a second novel in 1967, Ellison spent the remaining years of his life painstakingly attempting to re-create his work. The project was left unfinished at his death on April 16, 1994, in New York City. In 1999 an edition of the novel was published by his literary executor, John Callahan, with the title *Juneteenth*.

WILLIAM FAULKNER

(b. 1897–d. 1962)

The novels of William Faulkner rank among the most important books of the 20th century. For them Faulkner was awarded the 1949 Nobel Prize in Literature.

William Faulkner was born on Sept. 25, 1897, in New Albany, Miss. Early in his childhood the family moved to Oxford, Miss. There his father, Murry, was treasurer

William Faulkner in the 1950s. In addition to being an author, Faulkner was an accomplished horseman.
Mondadori/Getty Images

of the University of Mississippi. Faulkner's great-grandfather had fought in the Mexican War and the American Civil War, built a railroad, and written a best-selling novel, *The White Rose of Memphis*.

The oldest of four brothers, William attended Oxford schools but never graduated. Various contradictory accounts are given of his service in World War I. Back home after the war, he took a few courses at the university and began writing.

After two apprentice novels, Faulkner wrote six of his best books between 1929 and 1932. They are *Sartoris*, *The Sound and the Fury*, *As I Lay Dying*, *Sanctuary*, *These Thirteen* (short stories), and *Light in August*. Later works include *Intruder in the Dust*; *Go Down, Moses, and Other Stories*; *Knight's Gambit* (short stories); *A Fable*; *The Reivers*; and a trilogy on the Snopes family: *The Hamlet*, *The Town*, and *The Mansion*.

Faulkner wrote mostly about his hometown of Oxford, in Lafayette County, Miss. In his fiction the place was renamed Jefferson, in Yoknapatawpha County. The time in various stories ranges from pre–Civil War days to the early 1960s. Family names such as Sartoris, Snopes, De Spain, and

Compson recur in his work. His fiction re-creates more than a century of Jefferson life. People of all sorts—wealthy and poor, evil and good, slave and free—come into sharp focus in his writing. Despite his complex and sometimes confusing style, the "old verities and truths of the heart" are nearly always emphasized.

Faulkner won the Nobel Prize in Literature in 1949 and both the Pulitzer Prize and the National Book Award in 1954 for *A Fable*. He died on July 6, 1962, in Oxford.

F. SCOTT FITZGERALD

(b. 1896–d. 1940)

The novels and short stories of F. Scott Fitzgerald are famous for portraying the "lost generation" of the post–World War I era. They depict the rich, disenchanted youth of what he called the Jazz Age.

Francis Scott Key Fitzgerald was born in St. Paul, Minn., on Sept. 24, 1896, the only

Profile portrait of American author F. Scott Fitzgerald. Among his most notable works is The Great Gatsby. Hulton Archive/Getty Images

son of Edward and Mary Fitzgerald. His father was a descendant of Francis Scott Key, author of "The Star-Spangled Banner." Fitzgerald attended St. Paul Academy and the Newman School, in New Jersey. After entering Princeton University in 1913 he wrote for student publications. In November 1917 Fitzgerald left college to enlist in the Army. While stationed in Montgomery, Ala., he fell in love with Zelda Sayre.

Following his release from the army in 1919, Fitzgerald worked for an advertising agency in New York City for several months. After Zelda broke their engagement, he returned to St. Paul to rewrite a novel he had worked on when he was in the Army. The novel—*This Side of Paradise*—was published in 1920. The first chronicle of flaming youth, it brought Fitzgerald fame, money, and marriage to Zelda.

To maintain the luxurious life he and his wife liked to lead, Fitzgerald wrote at a furious pace. In 1920 he published *Flappers and Philosophers*, a volume of short stories. His second novel, *The Beautiful and Damned*, and the short-story collection *Tales of the Jazz Age* appeared in 1922. In 1924 the Fitzgeralds moved to Europe, where Fitzgerald wrote *The Great Gatsby*.

Typical of his work, *The Great Gatsby* glorified romance and disillusionment, and the dialogue was flawless. The narrator, Nick Carraway, is a young Princeton man who works as a bond broker in Manhattan. His neighbor in West Egg, Long Island, is Jay Gatsby, a self-made Midwesterner of considerable wealth. Nick watches as Gatsby is betrayed by his own dreams, which have been nurtured by a superficial society. The book was made into a film twice, in 1974 and 2013.

In 1930 Zelda suffered a mental breakdown. The family returned to the United States that same year. Fitzgerald's novel *Tender Is the Night* was published in 1934. It failed to sell, and Fitzgerald felt defeated. In 1936 he wrote about his emotional state in *The Crack-up*.

Fitzgerald went to Hollywood in 1937 to write scenarios for motion pictures. On Dec. 20, 1940, he suffered a fatal heart attack. He had begun a novel about Hollywood, called *The Last Tycoon*. The unfinished work, published in 1941, was another attempt to create his dream of the promises of American life and of a man who could realize them.

GUSTAVE FLAUBERT

(b. 1821–d. 1880)

Writing was not easy for the French novelist Gustave Flaubert. Because of his concern for form and precise detail, he often struggled for days searching for *le seul mot juste* ("the exactly right word"). He took five years to write *Madame Bovary*, his best-known work.

Gustave Flaubert was born on Dec. 12, 1821, in Rouen, France, where his father, Achille, was chief surgeon at the Hôtel-Dieu (hospital). His mother, Caroline Fleuriot, was the daughter of a doctor. Gustave was one of six children, only three of whom survived. While a student in Rouen, Gustave showed an early interest in literature. He and his friends acted in plays he had written when he was only 11. His first published work, *Song of Death*, appeared in the review *Le Colibri* in 1837.

At the insistence of his father, Flaubert went to Paris in 1841 to study law. In 1843, having failed his examinations and suffering from the onset of a nervous disorder, he decided to devote all his time to literature. After the deaths of his father and sister in 1846, a sizable inheritance enabled him to retire to the family estate at Croisset to write.

Flaubert sought to make literature a pure art. His aim was to write faultless, meticulously chiseled prose. "My head reels and throat aches with chasing after, slogging over, delving into, turning around, groping after, and bellowing, in a hundred thousand different ways, a sentence that I've at last finished," he said while working on *Madame Bovary*. In this novel, which tells of Emma Bovary's revolt against her middle-class environment, Flaubert revealed his own great contempt for the bourgeoisie. This group, he felt, was opposed to art and hated everything that it could not put to use.

When *Madame Bovary* first appeared—in 1856, as a magazine serial—Flaubert was brought to trial for publishing a morally offensive work. He was acquitted in 1857, and in the same year the novel came out in book form. Among his other works are the novels *Salammbô* (published in 1862), *L'Education sentimentale* (*Sentimental Education*, 1869), and *La Tentation de St.*

Antoine (*The Temptation of St. Anthony*, 1874). There are also a book of short stories, *Trois Contes* (*Three Tales*, 1877), and letters.

During his later years, Flaubert spent the winter in Paris, where he held literary gatherings. One of his guests was the writer Guy de Maupassant, whom he tutored for 10 years. Flaubert never married, instead devoting most of his life to caring for his mother and his niece. In 1875 he gave his fortune to save the niece's husband from bankruptcy. Flaubert died on May 8, 1880, at Croisset.

C.S. FORESTER

(b. 1899–d. 1966)

The British historical novelist and journalist C.S. Forester is best known as the creator of the character Horatio Hornblower, a British naval officer. Hornblower's rise from midshipman to admiral and peer during the Napoleonic Wars is told in a series of 12 novels.

Cecil Scott Forester was born on Aug. 27, 1899, in Cairo, Egypt. Abandoning medicine for writing, he achieved success with his first novel, a murder story entitled *Payment Deferred* (1926). The Hornblower series began with *Beat to Quarters* (1937; published in Great Britain as *The Happy Return*). His other books include *Brown on Resolution* (1929), *The Gun* (1933), *The General* (1936), and *The Ship* (1943). Many of his novels were adapted to motion pictures; most notable among these is *The African Queen* (1935), which in 1951 was made into an extraordinarily successful film starring Katharine Hepburn and Humphrey Bogart. Forester also wrote biographies and history books, including *The Last Nine Days of the Bismarck* (1959; also entitled *Sink the Bismarck!*). Forester described the genesis and progress of the Hornblower series in the self-revealing *Hornblower Companion* (1964).

Forester was a correspondent for *The Times* of London during the Spanish Civil War and the German occupation of Czechoslovakia. During World War II he worked as a propagandist in Great Britain and the United States. He died on April 2, 1966, in Fullerton, Calif. The last of the Hornblower books, *Hornblower and the Crisis* (1967), was published posthumously.

E.M. FORSTER

(b. 1879–d. 1970)

The works of the English novelist E.M. Forster have their roots in the Romantic movement: they urge humanity to maintain a close relationship with nature and, at the same time, to develop the imagination. These themes, albeit in a negative way, run through his best-known book, *A Passage to India* (1924; film, 1984), and they were expressed in a more positive way in his earlier novels, *The Longest Journey* (1907) and *Howards End* (1910; film, 1992).

Edward Morgan Forster was born in London on Jan. 1, 1879. He attended Tonbridge School at Kent and King's College, Cambridge. Upon leaving school, he decided to devote himself to writing. His early works, written in a plainer and more colloquial style than had been common in the 19th century, were filled with social commentary and criticisms of middle-class life in England, but they also gave indication of the deeper Romantic inclinations that dominated his later novels and short stories. Much of the inspiration for his writing came from travel, particularly in the Mediterranean area and India.

Forster's other novels include *Where Angels Fear to Tread* (1905) and *A Room with a View* (1908; film, 1986). Among his nonfiction works are *Alexandria: A History and a Guide* (1922; new edition, 1961), *Aspects of the Novel* (1927), *Two Cheers for Democracy* (1951), and *The Hill of Devi* (1953). He died in Coventry, Eng., on June 7, 1970.

WILLIAM GOLDING

(b. 1911–d. 1993)

The British novelist William Golding won the Nobel Prize for Literature in 1983 for his novels dealing with the human condition. His first book, *Lord of the Flies*, attracted a cult following, especially among the youth of the post–World War II generation.

William Gerald Golding was born in St. Columb Minor, near Newquay, Cornwall, Eng., on Sept. 19, 1911. He was educated at Marlborough Grammar School, where his father taught, and at Brasenose College, Oxford, receiving a bachelor of arts degree in 1935. After working in a settlement house and in small theater companies, he became a schoolmaster at Bishop Wordsworth's School in Salisbury in 1939. He joined the Royal

British writer William Golding is the author of the classic Lord of the Flies. Jean-Regis Rouston/Roger Viollet/Getty Images

Navy in 1940 and took part in World War II. After the war he resumed teaching at Bishop Wordsworth's.

Golding published *Lord of the Flies* in 1954 (film, 1963 and 1990). The story portrays a group of schoolboys isolated on a coral island who gradually abandon all moral constraints and revert to savagery, including ritualistic murder. The novel reflected Golding's belief that "man produces evil as a bee produces honey." It reportedly was rejected by 21 publishers before it finally appeared to lukewarm reviews. A paperback edition released in the United States in 1959, however, achieved cult popularity and a financial success that allowed Golding to quit teaching in 1961.

Golding continued to examine the essential violence and depravity of human nature in later novels, such as *The Inheritors* (1955), in which the last Neanderthals are destroyed by clever, weapon-wielding *Homo sapiens*, and *The Spire* (1964), a tale of vainglory and obsession in a medieval clergyman. *Pincher Martin* (1956) tells of the guilt-filled reflections of a naval officer who faces an agonizing death after his ship is torpedoed, and *Darkness Visible* (1979) follows a boy horribly burned in the London blitz during World War II. *Rites of Passage* (1980) won the Booker Prize and inspired two sequels, *Close Quarters* (1987) and *Fire Down Below* (1989). His other novels include *Free Fall* (1959), *The Pyramid* (1967), and *The Paper Men* (1984).

Golding was made Commander of the Order of the British Empire in 1966 and knighted in 1988. He died in Perranarworthal, Cornwall, on June 19, 1993.

GRAHAM GREENE

(b. 1904–d. 1991)

British author Graham Greene wrote so extensively that he forgot about a novel he wrote in 1944. Rediscovered in 1984, *The Tenth Man* was published a year later. Greene created a remarkable world of fiction from the tribulations, conflicts, and ideological battles of the 20th century.

Greene was born on Oct. 2, 1904, in Berkhamsted, Eng. After graduating from Oxford University he worked as a reporter for the *Nottingham Journal* and the *London Times*. After the publication of his first novel in 1929, he left the *Times* to be a writer and book and film critic. During World War II Greene worked for the foreign office. With the

Prolific British author Graham Greene. Louis Monier/ Gamma-Rapho/Getty Images

success of his books he settled on the French Riviera and divided his time between there and England.

Greene's first three novels were not significant, but he gained a literary reputation with *Stamboul Train* (1932; published in the United States as *Orient Express*). This was the first of many of his novels made into motion pictures. Among his other popular novels are *This Gun for Hire* (1936), *The Confidential Agent* (1939), *The Power and the Glory* (1940), *The Heart of the Matter* (1948), *The Third Man* (1949), *The End of the Affair* (1951), *Our Man in Havana* (1958), *A Burnt-Out Case* (1961), *The Comedians* (1966), *The Honorary Consul* (1973), and *The Human Factor* (1978).

Greene also wrote short stories, plays, and some nonfiction books, including *A Sort of Life* (1971) and *Ways of Escape* (1980), his autobiographies. He died on April 3, 1991, in Vevey, Switz.

THOMAS HARDY

(b. 1840–d. 1928)

Essentially a tragic novelist, Thomas Hardy wrote books that strike many readers as overly gloomy and pessimistic. A great novelist of the Victorian era, Hardy was also an accomplished poet.

Hardy was born on June 2, 1840, in Upper Bockhampton, near Dorchester in Dorsetshire, Eng. He passed most of his long life in this region of woodland, heath, and moor. It forms the setting of most of his writings, under its old name of Wessex. He attended local schools until he was 16, when he became an apprentice in an architect's office in Dorchester. In 1862 Hardy went to London to work as assistant to an architect. He had already begun to write verse and essays.

Hardy returned to Dorchester in 1867 because of ill health and soon began writing prose fiction for a living. His first really successful novel, published serially in 1874, was *Far from the Madding Crowd*. Others are *Under the Greenwood Tree* (1872), *The Return of the Native* (1878), *Tess of the D'Urbervilles* (1891), and *Jude the Obscure* (1895). His poetry includes *Wessex Poems* (1898) and *Time's Laughingstocks* (1909). *The Dynasts* (1903–08) is an epic drama in three parts.

Hardy viewed nature as a real power affecting the lives of his characters. His novels are realistic, but they resemble Greek tragedies in the way they show their characters as helpless victims of an unfeeling fate. Hardy's sympathy for his characters, even when they had done wrong, caused some of his works to be condemned as immoral.

In 1874 Hardy married Emma Lavinia Gifford, who died in 1912. In 1914 he married his secretary, Florence Emily Dugdale. He died in Dorchester on Jan. 11, 1928. His ashes were placed in Westminster Abbey, but his heart, at his request, was buried in Stinsford, near his birthplace.

NATHANIEL HAWTHORNE

(b. 1804–d. 1864)

Nathaniel Hawthorne wrote relatively little, but if he had written only his most famous work, *The Scarlet Letter*, his position as a major American writer would have been assured. The symbolism, psychological insight, and clarity of expression found in his writing have provided a model for generations of American writers.

Hawthorne was born on July 4, 1804, in Salem, Mass. His family, early Puritan

Portrait of American author Nathaniel Hawthorne. Library of Congress Prints and Photographs Division

settlers in America, had lived in Salem since the 1600s. One of his ancestors may have been a judge in the Salem witchcraft trials. Hawthorne's father, a ship's captain, died when Nathaniel was only four, and his mother became a virtual recluse. Hawthorne attended Bowdoin College in Brunswick, Me., where he befriended Franklin Pierce, who later became a president of the United States.

Hawthorne decided to become a writer, but until the 1840s he wrote little except for an amateurish novel, *Fanshawe*, published anonymously at his own expense in 1828. Some stories he sold to magazines were published as *Twice Told Tales* in 1837. The publication cost of the collection was underwritten by another of his college friends, Horatio Bridge. Hawthorne worked in the Boston Customhouse from 1839 to 1840, after which he spent a few months at Brook Farm, a cooperative agricultural community in West Roxbury, Mass. The Brook Farm experience was later described in his novel *The Blithedale Romance* (1852).

In 1842 Hawthorne married Sophia Peabody. The young couple spent the next three years in the Old Manse in Concord, where he wrote a second series of *Twice Told Tales*. *Mosses from an Old Manse*, published in

1846, describes their happy life in Concord. In 1845 Hawthorne returned to Salem and again worked in a customhouse. Relieved of that job in 1849, he found time to write. His best-known work, *The Scarlet Letter*, was published in 1850.

Moving from Salem to Lenox, Mass., Hawthorne wrote *The House of the Seven Gables*, which came out the following year. At Lenox he made the acquaintance of Herman Melville, a fellow writer whose novels show Hawthorne's influence. After a short stay in West Newton, Mass., the Hawthornes returned to Concord, where they purchased a house that had belonged to Bronson Alcott, renaming it Wayside.

In 1853 Franklin Pierce became president. He offered Hawthorne a consulship in Liverpool, Eng., a post that Hawthorne held until 1857. After resigning his position as consul, Hawthorne traveled in Europe, mostly in Italy. In 1860 the Hawthornes returned to their home in Concord. After *The Marble Faun*, published that year, Hawthorne wrote little. He aged rapidly and found it increasingly difficult to write. On May 19, 1864, while traveling with his friend Pierce, Hawthorne died in Plymouth, N.H.

ERNEST HEMINGWAY

(b. 1899–d. 1961)

A writer famous for his terse, direct style, Ernest Hemingway was also known for the way in which his own life mirrored the activities and interests of his characters. Many of his works show man pitted against nature, as in his favorite sports—hunting, fishing, and bullfighting. In others he tells of the experiences of wartime—man against man. The immediate appeal of his best writing probably stems from the fact that he wrote of things he knew intimately and that were important to him.

Ernest Hemingway was born on July 21, 1899, in Oak Park, Ill., a Chicago suburb. His father was a doctor. After high school Hemingway got a job as a reporter on the *Kansas City Star*. During World War I he tried to enlist in the armed forces but was rejected because of an old eye injury. He volunteered as an ambulance driver on the Italian front, and in 1918 he was badly wounded.

Ernest "Papa" Hemingway, known for his direct writing style and rugged, adventuresome lifestyle that informed his best works. Loomis Dean/Time & Life Pictures/Getty Images

After the war he settled in Paris, France, where he began to write fiction. He submitted his work for criticism to the poet Ezra Pound and to Gertrude Stein, a writer who served as friend and adviser to many writers of the time.

The first of many collections of stories, *In Our Time,* published in 1925, did not sell well. His novel *The Sun Also Rises*, which came out a year later, made his name known. It tells of young people in postwar Paris and their search for values in a world that in many ways has lost its meaning.

In *A Farewell to Arms* (1929), about war on the Italian front, Hemingway tells a love story that is interspersed with scenes of magnificent battle reporting. *To Have and Have Not* (1937) shows Hemingway's interest in social problems, an interest more fully realized in *For Whom the Bell Tolls* (1940), set during the Spanish Civil War. In *Across the River and into the Trees* (1950) an army officer dies while on leave. This novel is generally considered inferior to *The Old Man and the Sea* (1952), which won a Pulitzer Prize in 1953. Hemingway received the Nobel Prize for Literature in 1954.

Hemingway was a war correspondent in Spain, China, and Europe during World War II. He was married four times and had three sons. Toward the end of his life he suffered from anxiety and depression. He died on July 2, 1961, in his home in Ketchum, Idaho, of a self-inflicted shotgun wound.

HERMANN HESSE

(b. 1877–d. 1962)

In the 1960s many of the books written by Hermann Hesse became cult novels for the college-age generation. His emphasis on personal self-realization, youth's search for meaning, and Eastern mysticism gained him a temporary wide following.

Hesse was born in Calw, Ger., on July 2, 1877. He studied at Maulbronn Seminary to become a missionary but could not adapt to the work. Instead, he was apprenticed in a Calw tower-clock factory and later in a Tübingen bookstore. In 1904 he became a writer and brought out his first novel, *Peter Camenzind*. A visit to India in these years was later reflected in *Siddhartha* (1922), a poetic novel, set in India at the time of the Buddha, about the search for enlightenment.

During World War I, Hesse lived in neutral Switzerland, where he wrote pieces against militarism and nationalism and edited a journal for German war prisoners and internees. He became a permanent resident of Switzerland in 1919 and a citizen in 1923, settling in Montagnola.

Personal problems led him into psychoanalysis, an experience reflected in *Demian* (1919), a book about a troubled adolescent who achieves self-awareness. The novel made his reputation, and psychoanalytical themes continued to influence his later writing.

Among his other works are *Beneath the Wheel* (1906), *Steppenwolf* (1929), *Narcissus and Goldmund* (1930), and *Magister Ludi* (1943). He was awarded the Nobel Prize for Literature in 1946. He died in Montagnola, Switz., on Aug. 9, 1962.

VICTOR HUGO

(b. 1802–d. 1885)

The great French novelist and poet Victor Hugo created two of the most famous characters in literature—Jean Valjean, the ex-convict hero of *Les*

Misérables, and the hunchback Quasimodo in *The Hunchback of Notre Dame*. Known for the vast range and immense quantity of his output, Hugo was able during much of his long life to write as many as 100 lines of verse or 20 pages of prose each day.

Victor-Marie Hugo was born in Besançon, France, on Feb. 26, 1802, the son of an officer in Napoleon's army. In preparatory school, Hugo began to write. He won poetry prizes and wrote for a literary magazine he helped found. In 1821 the magazine failed. Hugo's mother died the same year. After a period of extreme poverty, Hugo was awarded an annual pension by Louis XVIII for his *Miscellaneous Odes and Poems*, published in 1822. He then married his childhood sweetheart, Adèle Foucher.

Between 1822 and 1832 Hugo established himself as a major literary figure in France. He wrote poetry, novels, and plays and became a leader in the Romantic movement. His novel *Notre Dame de Paris* was published in 1831. Translated as *The Hunchback of Notre Dame*, it became vastly popular in many countries. In 1832 his play *Le Roi s'amuse*, or *The King's Diversion*, on which Giuseppe Verdi later based his opera *Rigoletto*, was staged. Like so many of Hugo's works, *The Hunchback of Notre Dame* and *The King's Diversion* are criticisms of social and political injustice. Another reason for writing the plays was to provide parts for the young actress Juliette Negroni, who became his mistress in 1833 and was to be his companion for the rest of her life.

In 1841 Hugo was elected to the French Academy, and in 1849 he became a member of the National Assembly. An outspoken political opponent of Napoleon III, Hugo had to flee France in 1851. He remained in exile until 1870. During that time he wrote some of his finest works. In 1862 appeared *Les Misérables*, one of the most popular novels of all time. Hugo's wife died in 1868, and Negroni moved into his home.

After the fall of the empire in 1870, Hugo returned to Paris. There he lived the rest of his life as a literary idol. Huge crowds turned out to celebrate his 80th birthday in 1882. Hugo died in Paris on May 22, 1885, and is buried in the Panthéon there.

ZORA NEALE HURSTON

(b. 1891–d. 1860)

Writer, folklorist, and anthropologist Zora Neale Hurston celebrated the African American culture of the rural South. She wrote several novels as well as books of black mythology, legends, and folklore.

Hurston was born on Jan. 7, 1891, in Notasulga, Ala. Although she claimed to be born in 1901 in Eatonville, Fla., she moved with her family to Eatonville only as a small child. When she was 16 years old she joined a traveling theater company and ended up in New York City during the Harlem Renaissance. Hurston attended Howard University from 1921 to 1924 and in 1925 won a scholarship to Barnard College, where she studied anthropology under Franz Boas. She graduated from Barnard in 1928 and for two years pursued graduate studies in anthropology at Columbia University. She also conducted field studies in folklore among African Americans in the South. One result of these studies was the book *Mules and Men* (1935), a collection of

Portrait of Zora Neale Hurston. Among her most important works is Their Eyes Were Watching God. Library of Congress Prints and Photographs Division

folklore presented within the framework of a unifying narrative.

Hurston's background was also reflected in her novels, most of which incorporated elements of folklore to some degree. After studying in Haiti and Jamaica in 1936, she wrote *Their Eyes Were Watching God* (1937), which was widely considered her finest novel. It told the story of a young black woman's growth toward self-awareness and independence. Hurston's other novels were *Jonah's Gourd Vine* (1934), the tale of a black preacher; the allegorical *Moses, Man of the Mountain* (1939); and *Seraph on the Suwanee* (1948).

For a number of years Hurston was on the faculty of North Carolina College for Negroes (now North Carolina Central University) in Durham. She also was on the staff of the Library of Congress. *Dust Tracks on a Road* (1942), an autobiography, is highly regarded. Despite her early promise, by the time of her death Hurston was little remembered by the general reading public, but there was a resurgence of interest in her work in the late 20th century. Several other collections were published posthumously, including *Spunk: The Selected Stories* (1985), *The Complete Stories* (1995), and *Every Tongue Got to Confess* (2001), a collection of folktales from the South. In

1995 the Library of America published a two-volume set of her work in its series. Hurston died on Jan. 28, 1960, in Fort Pierce, Fla.

ALDOUS HUXLEY

(b. 1894–d. 1963)

The English writer and critic Aldous Huxley planned to become a doctor, but an illness that left him partially blind changed those plans. His passion for science served him well in his literary career, however. His novels, poems, essays, and critical works all display a keen interest in the workings of the natural world. He maintained his scientific outlook while also developing mystical beliefs and practices later in his life.

Born on July 26, 1894, in Godalming, Surrey, Eng., Aldous Leonard Huxley was the grandson of the biologist Thomas H. Huxley, brother of biologist and philosopher Julian, nephew of Mrs. Humphry Ward, and great-nephew of Matthew Arnold. While attending Eton he became partially blind owing to keratitis, but he retained enough eyesight to read with difficulty. He graduated from Balliol College, Oxford, in 1916. He published his first book in 1916 and worked on the periodical *Athenaeum* from 1919 to 1921. Thereafter he devoted himself largely to his own writing and spent much of his time in Italy until the late 1930s, when he settled in California.

In Huxley's pessimistic worldview, society had become callous and harsh. Many of his writings reflect his concern with the minimal potential for any individual in modern society. His brilliantly satirical early novels included *Crome Yellow* (1921) and *Antic Hay* (1923), both of which attack the London literary society of the post–World War I period. *Point Counter Point* (1928) and *Brave New World* (1932) are considered two of Huxley's finest works. *Brave New World* portrays a future society based on psychological conditioning. The vision is horrifying, and the novel is considered one of the best examples of anti-utopian literature. *Eyeless in Gaza* (1936), *Time Must Have a Stop* (1944), and *Brave New World Revisited* (1958) all reflect Huxley's interest in mysticism. His volumes of poetry include *Leda and Other Poems* (1920), *Apennine* (1930), and *The Cicadas and Other Poems* (1931).

Huxley traveled widely and spoke French, Spanish, Italian, and German fluently. In his search for a spiritual center, he experimented with LSD and other drugs and pursued studies of the occult. One of his important later works, *The Doors of Perception* (1954), describes his experiences with the hallucinogenic drug mescaline. He died on Nov. 22, 1963, in Los Angeles, Calif.

WASHINGTON IRVING

(b. 1783–d. 1859)

Essayist, historian, and writer of stories, Washington Irving was the first of the great American writers. Before his time Europe had regarded American authors chiefly as curiosities. It was quick to recognize this new writer, however, so graceful was his style and so fascinating and delicate his humor.

Washington Irving was born on April 3, 1783, in New York City, then a town of about 25,000, part of whom were Dutch and part English. It was from this town that he drew much of the material for his stories and sketches. While a boy, he spent many hours with dog and gun, rambling about the country regions that he later described. Sometimes he also wandered into the Dutch part of the city and listened to the quaint stories told by the Dutch descendants. At home he read a great deal in his father's large library. He was always cheerful, kindly, and sweet-natured, though a great part of his life was a struggle against ill health, grief, and work that he did not like. The day had not yet come when an American author could hope to support himself by his writing alone. There was no copyright law to protect his work.

Irving began the study of law, but his already delicate health was still further impaired by grief over the death of his fiancée. His family, therefore, sent him abroad, where he traveled in England, Holland, France, and Italy. When he returned, he wrote a humorous group of sketches entitled *Salmagundi*. A little later his burlesque *History of New York from the Beginning of the World to the End of the Dutch Dynasty* appeared. Irving soon went abroad again on business for his brothers. This time he met many famous writers in England and gained new inspiration and encouragement.

Washington Irving, the first of the great American writers, shown at work in a painting by Alonzo Chappel. Universal Images Group/Getty Images

He then set about writing in earnest. The first book he completed after this renewed effort was *The Sketch Book* (1819–20). Sir Walter Scott helped him sell the book to an English publisher, and Irving received $2,000 for it. *The Sketch Book* is the most widely known of Irving's works. It contains "Rip van Winkle" and "The Legend of Sleepy Hollow." In these he used the legends that the descendants of the old Dutch settlers had told him—the mysterious tale of the return of Hendrick Hudson and his men and the ghost story of the headless horseman. Other charming sketches by Irving are the essays on Westminster Abbey and the Shakespeare country.

Irving remained abroad for many years, traveling, writing, and serving in diplomatic posts for his country. While minister to Spain in 1842 he became interested in Spanish history. His studies there furnished his lively imagination with plenty of material for *The Alhambra* (1832) and other works.

The last 13 years of his life he spent at his home near Tarrytown on the Hudson River, a region his pen made famous. Irving died on Nov. 28, 1859, and is buried in Sleepy Hollow Cemetery, near the road where Ichabod Crane fled from the headless horseman.

HENRY JAMES

(b. 1843–d. 1916)

One of the most productive and influential American writers, Henry James was a master of fiction. He enlarged the form, was innovative with it, and placed upon it the mark of a highly individual method and style.

James was born on April 15, 1843, in New York City, the younger brother of the psychologist William James. He had two other brothers and one sister. His father, Henry, had inherited wealth, and the family enjoyed a life of leisure. The elder James lectured and wrote, largely about religious matters.

The James children were educated by private teachers, and Henry entered Harvard Law School in 1862. At first he seemed to have no definite idea of how he would use his many talents. He was just as interested in drawing and mathematics as he was in writing. At Harvard, however, under the influence of Charles Eliot Norton and William Dean Howells, James decided that literature would be his life's work.

From 1865 to 1869 he wrote criticism and

short stories. After much travel, he decided in 1875 to live in Europe. He went first to Paris but in 1876 settled in London. James received an honorary degree from Harvard in 1911 and one from Oxford in 1912. Angry at the United States for not entering World War I at its start, he became a British citizen in 1915.

Because he wrote of a society of sophistication and culture, James was accused of being a snobbish writer. He maintained, however, that it was only this kind of society that had the leisure to indulge in the delicate personal relationships in which he was interested. He wrote of these relationships with great psychological skill and in precise language, usually seeking to involve the reader in the thoughts and outlook of one character.

James wrote 20 novels, 112 shorter works, and 12 plays. The theme of much of his writing was the clash between the innocence and exuberance of the New World with the corruption and wisdom of the Old. His themes also included personal relationships, which he explored in *The Portrait of a Lady*, published in 1881, and social reform, of which he wrote in *The Bostonians* and *The Princess Casamassima* (both 1886). Some of his other works included *Daisy Miller* (1878), *Washington Square* (1880), *The Turn of the Screw* (1898), *The Wings of the Dove* (1902), and *The Ambassadors* (1903). James died on Feb. 28, 1916, in London. His ashes were taken to the United States and buried in Cambridge, Mass.

JAMES JOYCE

(b. 1882–d. 1941)

The Irish-born author James Joyce was one of the greatest literary innovators of the 20th century. His best-known works contain extraordinary experiments both in language and in writing style. In these works Joyce developed a technique of writing called "stream of consciousness." Using this technique, he ignored orderly sentence structure and attempted to reproduce in words the rambling processes of the human mind.

James Augustine Aloysius Joyce, one of several children of John Stanislaus Joyce, was born in Dublin, Ire., on Feb. 2, 1882. He was educated in Dublin at Jesuit schools and graduated from what was then known as Royal University. From boyhood he was fascinated by the sounds of words and by the rhythms of speech and song.

When he was in his early 20s, Joyce left Ireland to live in continental Europe. Although he divorced himself from both

Author James Joyce, noted for such classic works as Ulysses *and the stream-of-consciousness novel* A Portrait of the Artist as a Young Man. Lipnitzki/Roger Viollet/Getty Images

his homeland and his church, the major source of his literary inspiration was to be his early life in Dublin and the years he spent in its Jesuit schools. He lived for a time in Paris, France, and then settled in Trieste, Italy. Later he married Nora Barnacle, of Galway, Ire. Their son and daughter, George and Lucia, were born in Trieste.

Joyce, who is said to have known 17 modern and ancient languages, at times eked out a living as a language instructor. During World War I he took his family to Switzerland, which was neutral in the war. There his struggle for recognition as a writer was complicated by near-blindness. He underwent a long series of operations and had to wear a patch over one eye, which was damaged.

Chamber Music (1907), a book of poems, was Joyce's first published work. It was followed in 1914 by *Dubliners*, a collection of cruelly realistic short stories that deal with life in Joyce's native city. In 1916 Joyce's first full-length book using the stream-of-consciousness technique, *A Portrait of the Artist as a Young Man*, was published as a novel. It is an autobiographical work, with the central character Stephen Dedalus standing in for Joyce.

Stephen Dedalus is also a central character in *Ulysses*, an enormous work printed in book form in 1922 in Paris, where Joyce made his postwar home. The book recreates a single day in Dublin in 1904. The language of *Ulysses* is often as disjointed as the images in a dream. It is full of puns, slang, and metaphors. Portions of the book were considered obscene, and *Ulysses* was banned for many years in English-speaking countries.

Joyce's last work was *Finnegans Wake*, published in 1939 after parts of it had been serialized as *Work in Progress*. It is written almost in an invented language. His critics complained that Joyce had reached the ultimate in obscurity in the writing of *Finnegans Wake*.

Among other works by Joyce is a book of poems, *Pomes Penyeach* (1927). Part of the first draft of *A Portrait of the Artist as a Young Man* appeared in 1944 as *Stephen Hero*.

Joyce spent his last months in Switzerland, where he went in 1940 to escape the German occupation of France. He died in Zürich, Switz., on Jan. 13, 1941.

JACK KEROUAC

(b. 1922–d. 1969)

The writer who coined the term "beat generation" and became its leading

Portrait of Jack Kerouac, one of the leaders of the beat movement in 1950s America. Mondadori/Getty Images

spokesman was Jack Kerouac. The beat movement, a social and literary experiment, originated in the bohemian artists' colonies around San Francisco, Calif., and Greenwich Village in New York City in the late 1950s. Its adherents felt alienated from conventional society and often adopted unconventional styles of life.

Kerouac was born Jean-Louis Kerouac in Lowell, Mass., on March 12, 1922, to French-Canadian parents. He went to school in New York City and afterward served in World War II. After the war he became a wanderer, traveling through the United States and Mexico, unwilling to hold a steady job. His first novel, *The Town and the City*, published in 1950, was fairly well received.

Uncomfortable with conventional writing forms, Kerouac developed an unstructured, flowing, and spontaneous style that first made its appearance in *On the Road* (1957). This book, the bible of the beat movement, deals with the frenetic travels around the country of young people who, though poor, were in love with life, love, sex, drugs, jazz, and mysticism and completely rejected the standard values of the time.

The original manuscript of *On the Road*, a scroll written in a three-week blast in 1951, is legendary: composed of approximately 120 feet (37 meters) of paper taped together and fed into a manual typewriter, the scroll allowed Kerouac the fast pace he was hoping to achieve. He also hoped to publish the novel as a scroll so that the reader would not be encumbered by having to turn the pages of a book. Rejected for publication at first, it finally was printed in 1957.

The book drew public attention to the existence of a widespread subculture of artists, musicians, poets, and eccentrics that Kerouac had met on his travels. *On the Road* made him the culture hero of the movement. Other beat generation writers such as Allen Ginsberg and Lawrence Ferlinghetti also became prominent, especially as the beat movement was transformed into the counterculture of the 1960s. Like *On the Road*, all Kerouac's books, including *The Subterraneans* (1958), *Lonesome Traveler* (1960), and *Desolation Angels* (1965), are autobiographical in nature. Kerouac died in St. Petersburg, Fla., on Oct. 21, 1969.

D.H. LAWRENCE

(b. 1885–d. 1930)

In the English literature of the 20th century, few writers have been as original or as controversial as D.H. Lawrence. He was a man almost at war with the conventions, moral constraints, and technology of modern civilization. Much of his life was spent in the search for an ideal community of people in which to live. It was a search that failed in spite of his pilgrimages to such places as Italy, Ceylon (now Sri Lanka), Australia, and New Mexico. His quirks of personality, his wandering way of life, and the desire to explore the depths of human relationships brought originality to his novels and poems.

David Herbert Lawrence was born on Sept. 11, 1885, in the mining village of Eastwood, Nottinghamshire, Eng. With his mother's help he escaped the fate of becoming a miner and went instead to Nottingham High School and later to the University College at Nottingham. For several years he taught school, but when his first novel, *The White Peacock*, was published in 1911, he left teaching to concentrate on writing. This novel was followed by *The Trespasser* (1912) and the semiautobiographical *Sons and Lovers* (1913), as well as a volume of short stories, *The Prussian Officer and Other Stories* (1914). These works, well done but of a rather conventional nature, did not sell well but gave him a good reputation with literary critics.

Lawrence's conflict with the literary world began with the publication of *The Rainbow* (1915), which, with its sequel, *Women in Love* (1921), constitute his best work. These novels, intense psychological probings into human relationships, were condemned as obscene and their publication halted. The same fate met his most famous novel, *Lady Chatterley's Lover*, when it was first issued privately in 1928. The full text was not released to the public until 1959. Some few critics hailed his books as brilliant, while others condemned them as neurotic and indecent.

Lawrence's other published works include the novels *The Lost Girl* (1920), *Aaron's Rod* (1922), and *The Plumed Serpent* (1926); travel books, *Sea and Sardinia* (1921) and *Mornings in Mexico* (1927); and *Studies in Classic American Literature* (1923).

Lawrence seemed naturally restless and was constantly looking for the right place to live.

He and his wife, Frieda Richthofen Weekley, lived in Europe prior to World War I, spent the war in England, then traveled to Germany, Sicily, Sardinia, Ceylon, Australia, and eventually New Mexico. Lawrence died of tuberculosis in Vence, France, on March 2, 1930.

HARPER LEE

(b. 1926–)

Harper Lee, an American writer nationally acclaimed for her only novel, *To Kill a Mockingbird* (1960), was the daughter of the lawyer Amasa Coleman Lee. By all accounts, Amasa Lee was rather like the hero-father of her novel in his sound citizenship and warm-heartedness. The plot of *To Kill a Mockingbird* was based in part on his unsuccessful youthful defense of two African American men convicted of murder.

Nelle Harper Lee was born on April 28, 1926, in Monroeville, Ala. She attended the University of Alabama (spending a year as an exchange student at Oxford) but left for New York City before obtaining her own law degree. In New York she worked as an airline reservationist but soon received financial

Author of To Kill a Mockingbird, *Harper Lee, attending a 2005 awards dinner in Los Angeles.* Stephen Shugerman/ Getty Images

aid from friends that allowed her to write full-time. With the help of an editor, she transformed a series of short stories into *To Kill a Mockingbird.*

The novel was praised for its sensitive treatment of a child's awakening to racism and prejudice in the American South. It takes place in a small Alabama town in the 1930s and is told from the point of view of six-year-old Jean Louise ("Scout") Finch. She is the daughter of Atticus Finch, a white lawyer hired to defend Tom Robinson, a black man accused of raping a white woman. By observing the townspeople's reactions to the trial, Scout becomes aware of the hypocrisy and prejudice that exist in the adult world.

To Kill a Mockingbird received a Pulitzer Prize in 1961. It became a memorable film in 1962, starring Gregory Peck, who won an Oscar for his portrayal of Atticus. The story was filmed again in 1997.

After a few years in New York, Lee divided her time between that city and her hometown of Monroeville. In addition to her novel, she wrote a few short essays, including the 1983 "Romance and High Adventure," devoted to Alabama history. In 2007 Lee was awarded the Presidential Medal of Freedom.

In May 2013, Lee sued her literary agent over royalties derived from her classic novel. At that time, it was estimated that *To Kill a Mockingbird* had sold more than 30 million copies worldwide.

JACK LONDON

(b. 1876–d. 1916)

The novelist and short-story writer Jack London was, in his lifetime, one of the most popular authors in the world. After World War I his fame was eclipsed in the United States by a new generation of writers, but he remained popular in many other countries, especially in the Soviet Union, for his romantic tales of adventure mixed with elemental struggles for survival.

John Griffith London was born in San Francisco on Jan. 12, 1876. His family was poor, and he was forced to go to work early in life to support himself. At 17 he sailed to Japan and Siberia on a seal-hunting voyage. He was largely self-taught, reading voluminously in libraries and spending a year at the University of California. In the

American author Jack London, posing outdoors under a tree. The wilderness was a major character in many of London's best works. Time & Life Pictures/Getty Images

late 1890s he joined the gold rush to the Klondike. This experience gave him material for his first book, *The Son of the Wolf*, published in 1900, and for *Call of the Wild* (1903), one of his most popular stories.

In his writing career of 17 years, London produced 50 books and many short stories. He wrote mostly for money, to meet ever-increasing expenses. His fame as a writer gave him a ready audience as a spokesman for a peculiar and inconsistent blend of socialism and racial superiority.

London's works, all hastily written, are of uneven quality. The best books are the Klondike tales, which also include *White Fang* (1906) and *Burning Daylight* (1910). His most enduring novel is probably the autobiographical *Martin Eden* (1909), but the exciting *Sea Wolf* (1904) continues to have great appeal for young readers.

In 1910 London settled near Glen Ellen, Calif., where he intended to build his dream home, "Wolf House." After the house burned down before completion in 1913, he was a broken and sick man. He died on Nov. 22, 1916, in Glen Ellen. The official cause of death was listed as uremia.

BERNARD MALAMUD

(b. 1914–d. 1986)

The award-winning author Bernard Malamud drew from his Jewish heritage and his own experience to create novels and short stories that are warm, vivid, and universal. His characters endure extreme pain and hardship, but they are never enslaved by their circumstances.

Bernard Malamud was born in New York City on April 26, 1914. His parents were Russian Jewish immigrants who operated a grocery store. Educated at the City College of New York and Columbia University, he worked as a teacher in New York high schools from 1940 to 1949. He was a professor at Oregon State University from 1949 to 1961. He then taught at Bennington College in Vermont from 1961 until his death, with the exception of two years that he spent at Harvard University (1966–68).

Malamud's first novel was *The Natural*, published in 1952; the story was made into a movie starring Robert Redford in 1984. In *The Assistant* (1957), Malamud began to use his immigrant past in the story of a hardworking Jewish grocer. His collection of short stories *The Magic Barrel* (1958) earned him the National Book Award. *The Fixer* (1966) won both the National Book Award and the Pulitzer Prize for its vivid portrayal of anti-Semitism in tsarist Russia. Other works include *Pictures of Fidelman* (1969) and *The Stories of Bernard Malamud* (1983). Malamud died in New York City on March 18, 1986.

W. SOMERSET MAUGHAM

(b. 1874–d. 1965)

While studying to be a physician, Somerset Maugham wrote his first novel, *Liza of Lambeth*. Published in 1897, the year he completed his medical course, it is a story of life in the slums of London. The success of this book determined Maugham's career. He never practiced medicine.

William Somerset Maugham was born on Jan. 25, 1874, in Paris, France. His father was an English lawyer who was associated with the

Portrait of British author W. Somerset Maugham. Alfred Eisenstaedt/Time & Life Pictures/Getty Images

British Embassy in France. The boy's mother died when he was 8 and his father when he was 10. He was brought up by a childless uncle who was a clergyman in Kent, Eng. By the time he went to live with his uncle, young Maugham had read many books.

Maugham attended King's School in Canterbury, Kent, then went to the University of Heidelberg in Germany. On returning to England he entered the medical school at St. Thomas' Hospital in London.

The young author wrote rapidly but very well. He drew his material largely from the life around him. His early works include a number of successful plays, and in 1908 he had four plays running in London at the same time. His plays, mostly social comedies, include *A Man of Honour*, which opened in 1903, *Lady Frederick* (1907), and *Mrs. Dot* (1908).

Much of Maugham's philosophy is expressed in *Of Human Bondage* (1915), a novel based largely on his own experiences. This book, which is generally considered to be his best work, brought him recognition as a serious literary artist. It is ranked among the great novels of the 20th century. The plot is drawn from Maugham's youth and young manhood. The literary characteristics of this book are detachment, coolness, irony, keen observation, and revelation of motives—all of which show his excellent craftsmanship.

Among his other novels, one of the best is *The Moon and Sixpence* (1919). Maugham patterned this book on the life of the French painter Paul Gauguin. In 1930 he published the novel *Cakes and Ale*, an amusing story about a British author.

Maugham also wrote numerous short stories. Many appeared first in magazines and were later published in collections. Notable among these collections are *The Trembling of a Leaf* (1921) and *First Person Singular* (1931). *The Complete Short Stories*, in three volumes, was published in 1951. The most famous of his short stories is probably "Rain" (1921). In his short stories, as well as in his novels, Maugham explains his philosophy of life. The chief elements of his philosophy are the unpredictability of human actions and reactions and man's bondage to his emotions.

Maugham's later books include *The Razor's Edge* (1944), a novel about a man's efforts to find peace of soul, and *Then and Now* (1946), a historical novel about Niccolò Machiavelli. *The Razor's Edge* and *Of Human Bondage* were adapted as motion pictures, as were some of the writer's short stories.

Maugham also wrote considerable nonfiction. In 1938 he published *The Summing Up*, a commentary on his own writings and literary methods. *A Writer's Notebook* (1949) and *The Art of Fiction* (1955) are somewhat similar in content. In 1958 *Points of View*, a collection of essays, appeared.

In 1915 Maugham married Syrie Barnardo, but they were divorced in 1927. The writer spent much of his life in southern France. His home at St-Jean-Cap-Ferrat held a notable collection of modern art. Maugham died on Dec. 16, 1965, in Nice, France.

CARSON MCCULLERS

(b. 1917–d. 1967)

Although she left her home town of Columbus, Ga., when she was only 17, Carson McCullers wrote her plays, novels, and short stories against the background of the South where she had grown up. Loneliness and a sense of not belonging are themes that pervade her work, and the universal nature of these feelings has given her writing a lasting popularity.

Carson McCullers was born on Feb. 19, 1917, in Columbus. Her full name was Lula Carson Smith. She began to write at 15—plays at first, which she tried to persuade her family to act out. Her father, though reluctant to take part in these performances, encouraged her by buying her a typewriter.

After Smith graduated from Columbus High School, she went to New York City to study music. Unfortunately she lost the tuition money she had brought with her, so instead she worked at a variety of jobs and took a fiction workshop at New York University and a writing course at Columbia. In 1936 her story "Wunderkind" was printed in *Story* magazine. The next year she married Reeves McCullers, a writer whom she had met in Georgia.

In 1940 McCullers published her first novel, *The Heart Is a Lonely Hunter*. This book, which some critics consider to be her greatest achievement, is the story of a group of lonely people in a small Southern town and their relationships with each other.

With the profits from the book, she moved from Manhattan to a Brooklyn brownstone, which became a literary salon frequented by such diverse talents as Anaïs Nin, W.H. Auden, Leonard Bernstein, and Salvador Dali. Her second novel, *Reflections in a Golden Eye*, was published in 1941. About that time McCullers suffered a stroke, the first of three that eventually left her partially paralyzed.

Her novel *The Member of the Wedding*, which came out in 1946, tells the story of a lonely adolescent girl who wants to go along on her brother's honeymoon. A short novel, *The Ballad of the Sad Café*, was published together with several short stories in 1951. Following two further strokes she dictated from her hospital bed a dramatization of *The Member of the Wedding*. It opened on Broadway in 1950 and won the Drama Critics' Circle award as best play of the season. It was made into a motion picture in 1952. *The Square Root of Wonderful*, her second play, opened in New York in 1957.

Despite paralysis and further illness, McCullers finished her last novel, *Clock Without Hands*, in 1961. She also worked with Edward Albee on his 1963 dramatization of *The Ballad of the Sad Café*. McCullers died in Nyack, N.Y., on Sept. 29, 1967.

HERMAN MELVILLE

(b. 1819–d. 1891)

During his four years as a sailor and beachcomber in the South Pacific, Herman Melville gathered rich material for several novels. One of them was *Moby-Dick*, the story of Captain Ahab's vengeful search for the white whale that had maimed him. On the surface *Moby-Dick* can be read as an exciting adventure story. At a deeper level it is a profound study of man's struggle against the forces of evil.

Herman Melville was born in New York City on Aug. 1, 1819, the third of eight children. When the boy was 12, his father died. Herman was silent and slow. His mother considered him a dull child. He finished school when he was 15 and for two years worked at a series of jobs. Then he signed on as cabin boy aboard the *St. Lawrence*, bound for Liverpool, Eng. He left the *St. Lawrence* when it returned to New York, but he could not forget the sea.

In 1841 Melville took a berth as ordinary seaman aboard the whaler *Acushnet*. The ship left Fairhaven, near New Bedford, Mass., for a long voyage around Cape Horn

Portrait of Moby-Dick *author Herman Melville, by Joseph Eaton.* Apic/Hulton Fine Art Collection/Getty Images

and into the South Pacific. Melville discovered that the seafaring life was harsh and oppressive, and after 18 months he and a companion jumped ship at the Marquesas Islands. For several weeks they lived with the natives, then went aboard an Australian whaler. At Tahiti Melville went ashore, and for about a year he worked as a laborer. Finally he signed on as a seaman on the frigate *United States* and was discharged 14 months later when the ship docked at Boston.

Almost at once Melville began to set down his experiences. Within six years he published *Typee*, *Omoo*, *Mardi*, *Redburn*, and *White-Jacket*. He married and later moved his family from New York to a farm near Pittsfield, Mass. Nathaniel Hawthorne lived nearby, and the two authors became friends.

It was in Pittsfield that Melville wrote the book for which he is best known, *Moby-Dick*. The book tells the story of Captain Ahab's vengeful search for the white whale that had maimed him.

Melville threw himself into writing *Moby-Dick* and at the end was near collapse from mental exhaustion. It was published in 1851. Despite the toll writing the tale had taken, he at once began *Pierre*, which was published in 1852. Although his first books were popular, *Moby-Dick* and *Pierre* were attacked by the critics and virtually ignored by the public.

Melville's income from writing and farming was not enough to support his family, so he tried lecturing. At length he became a customs inspector in New York City, a post he held for 19 years. In the interim, he wrote several volumes of poetry and a number of short stories. One of the finest of these stories, "Benito Cereno," appeared in the collection *The Piazza Tales* (1856). He completed a short novel, *Billy Budd*, three months before his death on Sept. 28, 1891, in New York City, but it was not published until 1924.

HENRY MILLER

(b. 1891–d. 1980)

The candid autobiographical novels of U.S. writer and perennial bohemian Henry Miller had a liberating influence in mid–20th-century literature. Because of their sexual frankness, his major works were banned in Britain and the United States until the 1960s, but they were widely known earlier from copies smuggled in from France.

Born on Dec. 26, 1891, in New York City, Henry Valentine Miller was brought up in Brooklyn; he wrote about his childhood experiences there in *Black Spring* (1936). In 1924 he left his job with Western Union in New York to devote himself to writing. In 1930 he went to France. *Tropic of Cancer* (published in France in 1934 and in the United States in 1961) is based on his hand-to-mouth existence in Depression-ridden Paris. *Tropic of Capricorn* (France, 1939; U.S., 1961) draws on his earlier New York phase.

Miller's visit to Greece in 1939 inspired *The Colossus of Maroussi* (1941), a meditation on the significance of that country. In 1940–41 he toured the United States extensively and wrote a sharply critical account of it, *The Air-Conditioned Nightmare* (1945), which dwelt on the cost in human terms of mechanization and commercialization.

After settling in Big Sur on the California coast, Miller became the center of a colony of admirers, many of them like-minded writers of the beat generation. At Big Sur he produced his Rosy Crucifixion trilogy, made up of *Sexus*, *Plexus*, and *Nexus* (U.S. edition published as a whole in 1965).

It covers much the same period of Miller's life as *Tropic of Capricorn* and, together with that book, traces the stages by which the hero-narrator becomes a writer. The publication of the "Tropic" books in the United States provoked a series of obscenity trials that culminated in 1964 in a Supreme Court decision rejecting state court findings that the books were obscene.

Other important books by Miller are the essay collections *The Cosmological Eye* (1939) and *The Wisdom of the Heart* (1941). He was also a watercolorist who exhibited internationally; he wrote about art in *To Paint Is to Love Again* (1960). Various volumes of his correspondence have been published: with Lawrence Durrell (1963), to Anaïs Nin (1965), and with Wallace Fowlie (1975). Miller died on June 7, 1980, in Pacific Palisades, Calif.

VLADIMIR NABOKOV

(b. 1899–d. 1977)

The works of Russian-born American writer Vladimir Nabokov have been characterized as dealing with problems of art masked by allegory. The plots are devices by which he examined the nature of art itself.

Vladimir Vladimirovich Nabokov was born in Russia on April 23, 1899. His father was a prerevolutionary liberal politician and author. Young Nabokov grew up in St. Petersburg. His father opposed the Bolshevik government that came to power in 1917, and the family moved to Berlin, Ger., in 1919. The family went on to England, where Nabokov entered Cambridge University. He graduated in 1922, the same year his father was killed by a political assassin in Berlin. Nabokov rejoined his family and lived in Germany and France until 1940, when World War II was under way.

He had published collections of poetry in the early 1920s. His first novel, *Mashenka* (*Mary*), came out in 1926. It was followed by *King, Queen, Knave* (1928) and *The Defense* (1930). In 1925 he married Véra Slonim, a translator. Their son, Dmitri, was an opera singer and sports car racer and translated many of his father's works.

In 1940 Nabokov moved to the United States, where he taught literature. Most of his early work was written in Russian, but he also wrote novels in English—*The Real Life of Sebastian Knight* (1941), *Bend Sinister* (1947), *Pnin* (1957), *Pale Fire* (1962), *Ada* (1969), *Glory* (1971), and *Transparent Things* (1972)—as well as novellas and short stories.

Nabokov would probably have remained a fairly obscure novelist had it not been for his authorship of *Lolita*, published in 1955. Because of the furor this novel raised with critics and public alike, it became widely read, and it was eventually made into a play and a motion picture. The seemingly scandalous story line is simple: the antihero Humbert Humbert's passion for young girls. But the novel is in no way pornographic. It is a parody—true love is examined in the light of its opposite.

In 1945 Nabokov became a United States citizen. *Conclusive Evidence* (1951; revised as *Speak, Memory*, 1966) is an account of his early life. He died on July 2, 1977, in Montreux, Switz., where he lived from 1961.

FLANNERY O'CONNOR

(b. 1925–d. 1964)

The works of American novelist and short-story writer Flannery O'Connor are usually set in the rural American South, deal with alienation, and concern the relationship between the individual and God.

Mary Flannery O'Connor was born on March 25, 1925, in Savannah, Ga. She lived in Savannah until her adolescence, but the worsening of her father's lupus erythematosus (an autoimmune disease) forced the family to relocate in 1938 to the home in rural Milledgeville, Ga., where her mother had been raised. After graduating from Georgia State College for Women (now Georgia College & State University) in 1945, she studied creative writing at the University of Iowa Writers' Workshop.

Her first published work, a short story, appeared in the magazine *Accent* in 1946. Her first novel, *Wise Blood* (1952; film 1979), consists of a series of near-independent chapters, many of which originated in previously published

National Book Award winner Flannery O'Connor, whose works reflect her roots in the American South. Mondadori/Getty Images

short stories. With the publication of further short stories, first collected in *A Good Man Is Hard to Find, and Other Stories* (1955), she came to be regarded as a master of the form.

Her other works of fiction are a novel, *The Violent Bear It Away* (1960), and the short-story collection *Everything That Rises Must Converge* (1965). A collection of occasional prose pieces, *Mystery and Manners*, appeared in 1969. *The Complete Stories*, published posthumously in 1971, contained several stories that had not previously appeared in book form; it won a National Book Award in 1972.

Disabled for more than a decade by the lupus erythematosus she inherited from her father, which eventually proved fatal, O'Connor lived modestly, writing and raising peafowl on her mother's farm at Milledgeville. Her *Complete Stories*, published after her death, won the 1972 National Book Award. She died on Aug. 3, 1964, in Milledgeville, Ga.

GEORGE ORWELL

(b. 1903–d. 1950)

As a journalist and writer of autobiographical narratives, George Orwell was outstanding. But he will be

British author George Orwell, best known for the classic satires 1984 *and* Animal Farm. Popperfoto/Getty Images

remembered primarily for two works of fiction that have become 20th-century classics: *Animal Farm*, published in 1944, and *1984* (1949).

George Orwell is a pen name. His real name was Eric Arthur Blair, and he was born in 1903 at Montihari in Bengal, India, where his father was a minor British official. His family had social status but little money, a fact that influenced Orwell's later attitude toward the English class system and the empire's treatment of its subject peoples. In about 1911 the family returned to England. Blair was sent to school in Sussex, where he was distinguished both by his poverty and his intelligence. He later wrote of his miserable school years in *Such, Such Were the Joys* (1953). He attended Eton in the years 1917 to 1921 but decided against going on to a university. Instead he went to Burma (now Myanmar) as a member of the British imperial police.

His own poverty, plus his growing aversion to Britain's imperial policies, led him to resign from the government in 1928. He then spent several years among the poor and outcast of Europe and among the unemployed miners in the north of

England. These experiences are recounted in *Down and Out in Paris and London* (1933) and *The Road to Wigan Pier* (1937). Then Orwell went to Spain to report on the Spanish Civil War. His experiences in Spain are described in *Homage to Catalonia* (1938), one of his best books.

During World War II Orwell wrote for the British Broadcasting Company and worked as a literary editor for the *London Tribune*. The success of *Animal Farm* in 1944 allowed him to devote himself to writing. He bought a house on the island of Jura, where he wrote *1984*. By the time it was published, Orwell was already ill from the tuberculosis from which he died on Jan. 21, 1950, in London.

J.D. SALINGER

(b. 1919–d. 2010)

Although he is one of the most widely read authors in the English language, J.D. Salinger successfully kept himself out of the public eye for most of his career. His preference for seclusion made his life a matter of speculation among fans and his literary output a subject of controversy among critics.

Jerome David Salinger was born in New York City on Jan. 1, 1919. After studying at Columbia and New York universities, he turned to writing. His first short story appeared in *Story* magazine in 1940. After service in World War II his stories appeared regularly in the *New Yorker* magazine. Major recognition and a large following came with his novel, *The Catcher in the Rye*, published in 1951. This touching and humorous story about a rebellious teenager became a cult favorite among students. It was followed by *Nine Stories* (1953), *Franny and Zooey* (1961), and *Raise High the Roof Beam, Carpenters; and Seymour: An Introduction* (1963). The last two volumes contain stories about the Glass family.

Altogether Salinger produced 13 short stories and one novel. Some of the stories made use of his wartime experiences, as in "For Esmé—with Love and Squalor" (1950). "A Perfect Day for Bananafish" (1948) concerns the despair of veteran Seymour Glass. Salinger seemed at his best in dramatizing the lives of children.

Much of his work concerns the lost innocence of childhood. Salinger died on Jan. 27, 2010, in Cornish, N.H.

UPTON SINCLAIR

(b. 1878–d. 1968)

Deeply committed to social justice, Upton Sinclair believed in the power of literature to improve the human condition. He wrote more than 90 novels but is best remembered for *The Jungle* (1906), in which he described the wretched sanitary and working conditions in the Chicago meat-packing industry.

Upton Beall Sinclair was born on Sept. 20, 1878, in Baltimore, Md. He received a bachelor's degree from the City College of New York and did some graduate work at Columbia University. Sinclair published several unsuccessful novels before writing *The Jungle* for serialization in the socialist newspaper *Appeal to Reason*.

Publication of the novel placed Sinclair in the ranks of the early 20th-century muckraking writers who used their pens to expose corruption and social injustice. Although it was intended to arouse sympathy for the conditions of the workers, the novel instead led to the passage of the first food inspection laws in the United States.

Sinclair published numerous other protest novels, including *King Coal* (1917) and *The Profits of Religion* (1918). He also wrote 11 historical novels known as the Lanny Budd series. One of these novels, *Dragon's Teeth*, won the 1943 Pulitzer Prize. Throughout his life Sinclair was a vocal supporter of socialism. He died in Bound Brook, N.J., on Nov. 25, 1968.

JOHN STEINBECK

(b. 1902–d. 1968)

Winner of the 1962 Nobel Prize for Literature, the American author John Steinbeck is best remembered for his novel *The Grapes of Wrath*. Steinbeck's story of a family of farm workers migrating from Oklahoma to California describes the hopelessness of the Great Depression era.

John Ernst Steinbeck was born on Feb. 27, 1902, in Salinas, Calif. He took classes at Stanford University for several years but left without a degree. He worked as a laborer to support himself while he wrote. His experiences lent authenticity to his depictions of the lives of the workers in his stories. He spent much of his life in Monterey County, Calif., which later was the setting of some of his fiction.

Steinbeck's first novel, *Cup of Gold* (1929), was followed by *The Pastures of Heaven* (1932) and *To a God Unknown* (1933), none of which were successful. It was not until the publication of *Tortilla Flat* in 1935 that he attained critical and popular acclaim.

He followed this success with *In Dubious Battle* (1936) and the novella *Of Mice and Men* (1937). *The Grapes of Wrath* (1939) won a Pulitzer Prize and a National Book Award. In these works Steinbeck's proletarian themes are expressed through his portrayal of the inarticulate, dispossessed laborers who populate his American landscape. Both *Of Mice and Men* and *The Grapes of Wrath* were made into motion pictures.

After the best-selling success of *The Grapes of Wrath*, Steinbeck went to Mexico to collect marine life with the freelance biologist Edward F. Ricketts, and the two men collaborated in writing *Sea of Cortez* (1941), a study of the fauna of the Gulf of California. During World War II Steinbeck wrote some effective pieces of government propaganda, among them *The Moon Is Down* (1942), a novel of Norwegians under the Nazis, and he also served as a war correspondent. His immediate postwar work—*Cannery Row* (1945), *The Pearl* (1947), and *The Wayward Bus* (1947)—contain the familiar elements of his social criticism but are more relaxed in approach and sentimental in tone.

Some of Steinbeck's later works include *Burning Bright* (1950), *East of Eden* (1952), *The Winter of Our Discontent* (1961), and *Travels with Charley: In Search of America* (1962). He also wrote several motion-picture scripts, including adaptations of two of his shorter works—*The Pearl* and *The Red Pony.* Outstanding among the scripts he wrote directly for motion pictures were *Forgotten Village* (1941) and *Viva Zapata!* (1952). Steinbeck died in New York City on Dec. 20, 1968.

Author John Steinbeck, whose The Grapes of Wrath *won the Pulitzer Prize and a National Book Award.* Hulton Archive/Getty Images

ROBERT LOUIS STEVENSON

(b. 1850–d. 1894)

The history of English literature records few stories more inspiring than the life and work of Robert Louis Stevenson. He was a happy and gifted storyteller, poet, and essayist.

Robert Louis Balfour Stevenson was born on Nov. 13, 1850, in Edinburgh, Scot. Illness kept him bedridden throughout most of his childhood. He did not grow weary of his bed or resent it as a substitute for happy living. It was "the pleasant land of counterpane." His mother read to him the stories he loved to hear. He began to compose stories when he was six years old by dictating his ideas. A number of autobiographical poems from this time were later compiled as *A Child's Garden of Verses*, published in 1885.

No regular school attendance was possible in his childhood. When he grew older, he was able to take courses at Edinburgh University and to study engineering. It became plain, however, that he could not stand the activity of an engineer's life. He studied law and was admitted to the bar in 1875, but he had no liking for law. He decided to develop his natural gift for speech and writing.

While spending the winter of 1873–74 on the Riviera because of a severe spell of bad health, he began contributing essays to periodicals. Even in these early works he showed an ability to write in a charming, easy style. In 1874 he joined the Savile Club (then known as the New Club) in London and made friends among leading literary men.

After being admitted to the bar, he spent several years wandering through France, Germany, and Scotland for his health. These journeys were recorded in *An Inland Voyage* in 1878 and *Travels with a Donkey* in 1879. Readers were charmed by Stevenson's delightful conversational manner and by the graceful flow of his style. They did not realize how hard a schooling he had given himself in the art of writing.

All his life he labored for perfection in his writing. With the publication of his first long tale, *Treasure Island*, in 1883, Stevenson became widely popular. He wrote many essays, poems, and short stories and then in

Scottish writer Robert Louis Stevenson penned several tales of adventure and intrigue that are taught and read to this day. Hulton Archive/Getty Images

1886 another absorbing story of adventure, *Kidnapped*. Stevenson did not concern himself with the problems of life and society, the mysteries of thought and conduct into which George Eliot and Thomas Hardy and other realists of the 19th century delved so deeply. He returned to the pure romanticism of Sir Walter Scott—the love of a story for its own sake, the delight in adventure, the spirit of eternal youth.

Stevenson's best-known works include the essay collections *Virginibus Puerisque* (1881) and *Familiar Studies of Men and Books* (1882); the short-story collections *New Arabian Nights* (1882) and *The Merry Men and Other Tales and Fables* (1887); and the novels *The Silverado Squatters* (1883), *Prince Otto* (1885), *The Strange Case of Dr. Jekyll and Mr. Hyde* (1886), *The Master of Ballantrae* (1889), *The Wrecker* (1892), *The Ebb Tide* (1894), and *The Body-Snatcher* (1895). His last work, the unfinished novel *Weir of Hermiston*, was published posthumously in 1896 and is considered by many scholars to be his finest work.

Stevenson developed tuberculosis during a visit to the United States in the 1870s and may have died had it not been for a woman named Fanny Van de Grift Osbourne, who nursed him back to health. In 1880 they were married, and Stevenson returned with his wife and stepchildren to Scotland. He could not stand the severe climate of Scotland, however, and for years he wandered from place to place in search of a climate where he might live and work. He settled with his family in one of the Samoan Islands (Upolu) in the South Pacific, where he bought a large estate. The people on the island called him "Tusitala" (teller of tales).

On Dec. 3, 1894, while talking on the veranda of his house at Vailima, he had a stroke and died within a few hours. The Samoans carried his body to Mount Vaea, cutting a path to the summit with their knives and axes. There they buried him, and there he lies today in a windswept solitude overlooking the Pacific, with one of his verses for an epitaph:

Under the wide and starry sky,
Dig the grave and let me lie.
Glad did I live, and gladly die,
And I laid me down with a will.
This be the verse you grave for me:
"Here he lies where he longed to be.
Home is the sailor, home from the sea,
And the hunter home from the hill."

JONATHAN SWIFT

(b. 1667–d. 1745)

When Jonathan Swift wrote *Gulliver's Travels*, he intended it as a satire on all of humankind. He proposed, in his own words, "to vex the world rather than divert it." Instead, people enjoyed his story and gave it to children to read. Today most readers know this quite ferocious indictment of human nature only as an amusing tale for children.

Jonathan Swift was born on Nov. 30, 1667, in Dublin, Ire. His parents were English. Born a few months after his father's death, Swift was dependent upon an uncle. He attended the prestigious Kilkenny School in Ireland and was admitted to Trinity College, Dublin, in 1682.

In 1689, Swift traveled to England. Through his uncle he was introduced to Sir William Temple, a retired Anglo-Irish statesman. Swift became a secretary to Temple and lived at his house off and on for 10 years. It was there that he met Esther Johnson, whose mother was Temple's housekeeper. When Swift first met Esther she was only 8 years old—14 years younger than he. He taught her to read and write, and throughout her life she was his closest friend. After her death she was known to the world as Stella, a nickname Swift gave her. They may have been secretly married as early as 1716, but they probably never lived together as husband and wife.

During the first years with Temple, Swift wrote a few poems that the poet John Dryden, Swift's cousin, is said to have told him were not good. Swift turned away from writing poetry, which he did not think of as a profession. Between 1696 and 1697 he wrote his first important satires, *A Tale of a Tub* and "The Battle of the Books." He did not publish them, however, until 1704.

In 1710, Swift, up to that time a Whig, went over to the Tories. This led to his employment by the newly seated Tory ministry. The Tory ministers set themselves to destroy Whig power and bring peace. They used Swift to arouse public opinion against the Whigs by his writings. In the Tory *Examiner*, as well as in pamphlets and verse, Swift carried on a vigorous campaign against the Whigs for their refusal to view the interests of Britain as a whole. In all this Swift wrote anonymously.

Swift made friends among the Tories: the witty and spiteful Alexander Pope; John Gay, author of *The Beggar's Opera*; and John Arbuthnot, physician to Queen Anne. With some others they formed the Scriblerus Club. Together they planned to write the burlesque memoirs of the imaginary Martinus Scriblerus. Although this project was barely begun and outlined, it was the seed of *Gulliver's Travels*.

During these years, Swift sent Stella in Dublin a day-by-day account of everything he did. This *Journal to Stella*, written with no thought of publication, is a fascinating record not only of Swift's life but also of London society and politics in Queen Anne's reign. It remains one of the great diaries of English literature.

In 1729, Swift published the most terrible of his satiric pamphlets against the Whigs. The gist of *A Modest Proposal* was that the Irish poor raise their children as food for the tables of the wealthy, particularly their English landlords.

After 1720 Swift again took up the Scriblerus memoirs, and by 1725 he had finished *Gulliver's Travels*. When the book was published in 1726, the author's name did not appear on the book because of

the political satire contained therein. The title page read "Travels into several remote Nations of the World, by Lemuel Gulliver . . ." Many people accepted this as fact. Travel books of the time told many tales that were no more strange than the imaginary adventures of Gulliver. One sea captain even claimed that he knew Captain Gulliver well. Other readers condemned the book as full of exaggerations.

From its first appearance *Gulliver's Travels* delighted its readers instead of shocking them. In spite of his bitterness, Swift took a dry delight in making his narrative sound real even when it was fantastic. Children could enjoy the marvelous adventures of a traveler among pygmies and giants, on a flying island, and in a country where horses talk. *Gulliver's Travels* soon became a children's classic.

After Stella died in 1728, Swift was lonely. He suffered from attacks of deafness and dizziness, and for the last three years of his life some people thought that he was insane. He died in Dublin on Oct. 19, 1745, and was buried in St. Patrick's Cathedral, beside Stella.

WILLIAM MAKEPEACE THACKERAY

(b. 1811–d. 1863)

Next to Charles Dickens the greatest Victorian English novelist is William Makepeace Thackeray. His *Vanity Fair* is the first novel in English to show a woman who is neither very good nor very bad but only very human. His *Pendennis* is the story of an all-too-human man. *The History of Henry Esmond Thackeray* blends fact and fiction into a believable historical novel; in *The Newcomes* he used his own knowledge of the social world of England and India.

Thackeray was born on July 18, 1811, in Calcutta, India. He was the only child of Richmond and Anne Becher Thackeray. His father, who worked for the East India Company, died when the boy was four. At six young William was sent back to England to go to school. He spent six years at the famous Charterhouse school. Later he attended

Trinity College, Cambridge, for a year and a half. As a child Thackeray was nearsighted and frail. He grew up to be six feet four inches tall, broad and heavy. His otherwise handsome face was marred by a nose broken at school.

In 1830–31 Thackeray spent a year in continental Europe, then returned to London to study law. He soon turned to art and went to Paris in 1834 for art training. He also served as Paris correspondent for a short-lived paper owned by his stepfather.

In Paris he married Isabella Shawe in 1836. They had three daughters, although one died in infancy. The birth of their youngest child affected Mrs. Thackeray's mind. Thackeray placed her in a home and set about earning a living for his daughters. Money from his father's estate had been squandered. His need for funds made him a literary hack, turning out reviews, articles, and magazine stories.

Among the assumed names he used was Michael Angelo Titmarsh (Michelangelo also had a broken nose). Under this name he published several volumes of sketches and stories in the 1840s. He was on the staff of *Punch*, the famous weekly, for 10 years.

Vanity Fair, his first novel, was published as a magazine serial, starting in 1846. It was ignored in the beginning, but soon readers were eagerly waiting for the next issue. It was the beginning of a well-deserved popularity.

Most of Thackeray's works were published as serial stories before they appeared in book form. This list, in which most of the titles are shortened, arranges his chief works in order of their publication: *Catherine*, *Barry Lyndon*, *The Book of Snobs*, *Vanity Fair*, *The Great Hoggarty Diamond*, *Pendennis*, *Rebecca and Rowena*, *The Kickleburys on the Rhine*, *Henry Esmond*, *The English Humourists*, *The Newcomes*, *The Rose and the Ring*, *The Virginians*, *The Four Georges*, *The Adventures of Philip*, and *Roundabout Papers*.

Thackeray made two lecture tours of the United States (1852–53 and 1855–56). These were successful, but he was never very happy about lecturing. He acted as editor of the *Cornhill Magazine*, 1860–62, but he was uneasy about this work as well. He hated to refuse contributions, even though he could not use them in the magazine. He died suddenly on Dec. 24, 1863, in London.

LEO TOLSTOY

(b. 1828–d. 1910)

The great novels of the Russian writer Leo Tolstoy capture the vastness of the Russian landscape and the complexity of its people. His massive *War and Peace* is regarded as a milestone in the development of the Western novel and spread his social and moral ideals to all parts of the world.

Leo Nikolayevich Tolstoy was born in the village of Yasnaya Polyana in the central Russian province of Tula. The date was Sept. 9, 1828, or August 28 according to the calendar being used at the time. Tolstoy's parents, Count Nikolay Ilich Tolstoy and Princess Mariya Nikolayevna Volkonskaya, were married in Moscow in 1822. They came from distinguished families of the Russian nobility. The couple moved to her family's estate at Yasnaya Polyana in 1823 with their first child, Nikolay. There Sergey, Dmitry, and Leo were born. The household was a happy one. Tolstoy re-created many of the scenes of his childhood in his writings.

Tolstoy's mother died in 1830 after the birth of a daughter, Mariya. Seven years later the count died. Relatives and friends cared for the orphans until they were taken to Kazan to live with an aunt in 1841. Leo showed intelligence, sensitivity, and imagination early in life. In 1836 a tutor had predicted literary fame for the boy.

Tolstoy entered the University of Kazan in 1844. He soon became dissatisfied with the educational system. His study of the French philosopher Jean-Jacques Rousseau encouraged his rebellious attitude and greatly influenced his moral, social, and educational beliefs. In 1847 Tolstoy left the university, saying that he had lost faith in religion and prayer.

In 1851, tired of the irresponsible lifestyle he had chosen, he accompanied his brother Nikolay, a military officer, to the Caucasus. There Leo joined the army in 1852. In 1854 he was commissioned an officer and served bravely in the Crimean War until 1856. He used and described his army experiences in many of his stories and novels.

Tolstoy's first published work appeared in the Russian magazine *Contemporary* in 1852. It was based on his own memories and was titled "Childhood." More stories and accounts of the Crimean campaign were soon published. He was a well-known author by 1856. In 1862, he married Sofya Andreyevna Bers. They lived in Yasnaya Polyana for the next 48 years and had 13 children.

Tolstoy's epic novel of Russian life during the time of Napoleon, *War and Peace*, was completed in 1869. His other famous works include *Anna Karenina* (1877); the novella *The Death of Ivan Ilyich* (1886); *The Power of Darkness*, a play written in 1886; *Master and Man* (1895); and *Resurrection* (1899).

After 1879 Tolstoy changed his way of life. He determined to live by a code of non-violence, universal love and forgiveness, and simplicity. This moral crisis was recorded in his essay "Confession" (1879). His writings became increasingly devoted to his beliefs. Two of them were *The Kingdom of God Is Within You* (1893) and *What Is Art?* (1897). Tolstoy's creed attracted many followers, who were called Tolstoyans.

Tolstoy was often in opposition to the Russian government and the church. Many of his works were censored, and his followers were persecuted. He was, however, protected from harm by his worldwide fame and the love the Russian people had for him.

Tolstoy and his family were driven apart by conflicts in their beliefs. At the age of 82 he left Yasnaya Polyana, intending never to return. He became ill on the journey and died on Nov. 20 (Nov. 7), 1910, at the railroad station of Astapovo in Ryazan Province.

Russian author Leo Tolstoy sharing a story with his grandchildren.
Universal Images Group/Getty Images

ANTHONY TROLLOPE

(b. 1815–d. 1882)

English author Anthony Trollope's tales of the imaginary cathedral town of Barchester are peopled with unforgettable human beings. Trollope depicted the clerical society and political life of Victorian times with both humor and pathos.

Anthony Trollope was born on April 24, 1815, in the Bloomsbury district of London. His father was an intellectual but a hopeless failure at everything. His mother, Frances Milton Trollope, was a well-known author in her own right and the strength and support of the family.

At school, young Anthony had a miserable life because of his family's monetary hardships. He had no spending money, and his school bills were unpaid. In 1834, when Trollope was 19, the sheriff seized the family's possessions for debts. Anthony and his sisters managed to hide a few of their mother's treasures and flee to Belgium.

In 1834 a family friend obtained for Anthony a position as clerk in the London General Post Office. The next seven years were as lonely and poverty-stricken as ever. In 1841 he went to Ireland as a traveling inspector for the post office. At last good fortune came to him. He had more money and made friends. He learned to love the sport of hunting, which he vividly describes in his books. He married Rose Heseltine in 1844, and they had two sons.

Trollope traveled in the rural districts of Great Britain, and he went on special missions to Egypt and the West Indies. He is credited with regulating rural mail deliveries and foreign mails and originating the pillar-box (corner mailbox). He began to write of the people and things he observed, rising early every morning to write before work.

The *Cathedral Stories*, or the *Chronicles of Barsetshire*, are Trollope's best-known books. They include *The Warden* (1855), *Barchester Towers* (1857), *Doctor Thorne* (1858), *Framley Parsonage* (1861), *The Small House at Allington* (1864), and *The Last Chronicle of Barset* (1867). These were condensed for a television series in 1982 called *The Barchester Chronicles*.

Can You Forgive Her? (1864) introduced the political, or parliamentary, novels dramatized on television in 1975 as *The Pallisers*. Other popular books are *The Three Clerks* (1858), *Orley Farm* (1862), and *The Claverings* (1867).

Trollope died on Dec. 6, 1882, in Harting, Sussex. His autobiography, edited by his son Henry M. Trollope, was published posthumously the following year.

MARK TWAIN

(b. 1835–d. 1910)

A onetime printer and Mississippi River boat pilot, Mark Twain became one of America's greatest authors. His *Tom Sawyer*, *Huckleberry Finn*, and *Life on the Mississippi* rank high on any list of great American books.

Mark Twain was born Samuel Langhorne Clemens on Nov. 30, 1835, in the small town of Florida, Mo. His father was a hard worker but a poor provider. The family moved to Hannibal, Mo., on the Mississippi, when young Clemens was four years old. It was in this river town that he grew up, and from it he gathered the material for his most famous stories.

His father died when Samuel was 12, and the boy was apprenticed to a printer. This was the first step toward his career as a writer. In 1850 his older brother, Orion, began to publish a weekly newspaper. A year later he bought the *Hannibal Journal*, and Sam and his younger brother Henry worked for him. Sam became more than competent as a typesetter, but he also occasionally contributed sketches and articles to his brother's paper. Some of those early sketches, such as *The Dandy Frightening the Squatter* (1852), appeared in Eastern newspapers and periodicals. In 1852, acting as the substitute editor while Orion was out of town, Clemens signed a sketch "W. Epaminondas Adrastus Perkins." This was his first known use of a pseudonym, and there would be several more before he adopted, permanently, the pen name Mark Twain.

Clemens left Hannibal in 1853, working briefly as a typesetter in St. Louis before traveling to New York City to work at a large printing shop. From there he went to Philadelphia and on to Washington, D.C. He continued to write, though without firm literary ambitions, occasionally publishing letters in his brother's new newspaper.

In 1857 he apprenticed himself to a riverboat pilot. He became a licensed pilot himself, working for two and a half years

Portrait of American author Samuel Langhorne Clemens, more popularly known as Mark Twain. Library of Congress, Washington, D.C. LC-USZ62-112728

at his new trade along the Mississippi River. He wrote of these years in *Life on the Mississippi* (1883).

The Civil War ended his career as a pilot. Clemens went west to Nevada and soon became a reporter on the Virginia City newspaper. There he began using the pen name Mark Twain. It is an old river term meaning two fathoms, or 12 feet (4 meters), of water depth.

In 1864 he went to California, to the Tuolumne foothills, to do some mining. It was there that he heard the story of a jumping frog—a widely known story that was new to Clemens. He took notes and, when he was invited to contribute something for a book of humorous sketches, decided to write up the story. *Jim Smiley and His Jumping Frog* arrived too late to be included in the volume, but it was published in the *New York Saturday Press* in November 1865 and was subsequently reprinted throughout the country. "Mark Twain" had acquired sudden celebrity.

Clemens was sent to the Sandwich Islands (now Hawaii) as a reporter, and on his return he began lecturing. He was soon on a tour of the Mediterranean and

the Holy Land. From this came *The Innocents Abroad* (1869), which made him famous.

In 1870 Clemens married Olivia Langdon. He began turning out a new book every few years. *Roughing It*, a novel based on his experiences in California and Nevada, written with his friend Charles Dudley Warner, was published in 1872. Twain's first attempt at a novel was *The Gilded Age* (1873). He followed that with *Old Times on the Mississippi* (later *Life on the Mississippi*), which appeared in the *Atlantic Monthly* in installments in 1875.

Tom Sawyer (1877), which recounts the mischievous adventures of a boy growing up along the Mississippi River, was colored by a nostalgia for childhood and simplicity. The continuing popularity of *Tom Sawyer* (it sold well from its first publication, in 1876, and has never gone out of print) indicates that Twain could write a novel that appealed to young and old readers alike.

In the summer of 1876, while staying with his in-laws Susan and Theodore Crane on Quarry Farm overlooking Elmira, N.Y., Clemens began writing what he initially called "Huck Finn's Autobiography." Huck had appeared as a character in *Tom Sawyer*, and Clemens decided that the untutored boy had his own story to tell. *Huckleberry Finn* was written in fits and starts over an extended period and would not be published until 1885. During that interval, Twain often turned his attention to other projects, only to return again and again to the novel's manuscript. The controversial *Huckleberry Finn*, which is periodically banned in schools or libraries because of alleged racial overtones, can be read by children, but it is not a child's book. It has elements of heartbreak and wisdom that can be appreciated best by adults.

Other of Clemens's chief works include *The Celebrated Jumping Frog of Calaveras County*, a collection published in 1867; *A Tramp Abroad* (1880); *The Prince and the Pauper* (1882); *A Connecticut Yankee in King Arthur's Court* (1889); *The Tragedy of Pudd'nhead Wilson* (1894); and *Personal Recollections of Joan of Arc* (1896).

In 1884, Clemens bought a publishing firm in Hartford, Conn. He earned much money writing and lecturing as well as in his publishing house, but he spent it on high living and unsuccessful investments.

He lost a fortune promoting a typesetting machine. By 1894 his publishing company had failed, and he was bankrupt. He set out on a world lecture tour to retrieve his fortune, and by 1898 his debts were paid.

In his last years, Clemens traveled and spoke much but wrote little. He died on April 21, 1910, in Redding, Conn. His *The Mysterious Stranger* (1916), *Mark Twain's Notebook* (1935), and *Autobiography* (1959) were printed posthumously.

EVELYN WAUGH

(b. 1903–d. 1966)

English author Evelyn Waugh was considered by many to be the preeminent satirical writer of his day. Combining scathing social criticism and black comedy, his novels lampoon the manners and morals of aristocratic British society and its institutions.

Evelyn Arthur St. John Waugh was born on Oct. 28, 1903, in London, Eng. Evelyn's father, Arthur Waugh, was a publisher. His elder brother, Alec Waugh, became a novelist and travel writer. Waugh attended Lancing College, Sussex, and Hertford College, Oxford. After leaving Oxford he spent brief periods as an art student and a schoolmaster before traveling throughout the world.

Waugh's first published writings include *The World to Come: A Poem in Three Cantos*, a juvenile piece published in 1916, and *PRB: An Essay on the Pre-Raphaelite Brotherhood 1847–1854* (1926). His early novels won acclaim for their sophisticated wit and technical innovation. His first popular success was *Decline and Fall* (1928), a scathing satire based on his teaching experiences. In that same year he published a biography of the artist Dante Gabriel Rossetti.

A string of satirical novels published in the 1930s include *Vile Bodies* (1930), *A Handful of Dust* (1934), and *Scoop* (1938), the last of which was inspired by Waugh's experiences as a reporter covering the Italo-Ethiopian War in 1935–36. He also published several travel books, including *Labels: A Mediterranean Journal* (1930); *Remote People* (1931), based on his travels in Africa; *Ninety-Two Days* (1934), which was about South America; *Waugh in*

Evelyn Waugh, known primarily for his satirical writings.
Topical Press Agency/Hulton Archive/Getty Images

Abyssinia (1936); and *Robbery Under Law: The Mexican Object Lesson* (1939). *A Tourist in Africa* (1960) was Waugh's last travel book.

Waugh converted to Roman Catholicism in 1930, and after the conversion he began to introduce religious themes into his writings. The most notable example of this development is *Brideshead Revisited* (1945), considered by many critics to be Waugh's best novel. The book concerns the declining fortunes of an aristocratic Roman Catholic family, some of whom recover their faith despite significant lapses. The book was adapted for a television series in 1981. Set in ancient Rome, *Helena* (1950) is a historical novel about the mother of Emperor Constantine that also explores theological issues. *The Loved One* (1948), a return to satire, ridicules the funeral industry in Hollywood, Calif.

During World War II Waugh joined the Royal Marines and the Royal Horse Guards, serving in North Africa, Crete, and Yugoslavia. Upon his discharge from the military Waugh retired to Somerset, Eng., where he lived until his death. His *Sword of Honor* trilogy, a satire based on his experiences in World War II, includes *Men at Arms* (1952), *Officers and Gentlemen* (1955), and *Unconditional Surrender* (1961); the trilogy was published together in 1965. The frankly autobiographical *Ordeal of Gilbert Pinfold* (1957) tells the story of a middle-aged novelist who suffers a mental collapse but eventually recovers. *A Little Learning* (1964), Waugh's unfinished autobiography, describes his youth and education.

Waugh died on April 10, 1966, in Somerset. His diaries, published in 1976, reveal the identities of many individuals who inspired characters in his fiction. Several collections of his letters were also published after his death.

EDITH WHARTON

(b. 1862–d. 1937)

The upper-class society into which Edith Wharton was born provided her with abundant material for plotting her novels and short stories. Her major literary model was Henry James, a close friend in her later years. Like him, she lived a great part of her life in Europe, rarely returning to the United States after 1907.

Wharton was born Edith Newbold Jones in New York City on Jan. 24, 1862. She was educated by private tutors at home and in Europe. She married Boston banker Edward Wharton in 1885. Her first novel, *The Valley of Decision*, was published in 1902. Critical acclaim came with *The House of Mirth* in 1905. It analyzed the aristocratic society she knew and its reaction to social change.

A similar theme was evident in *The Custom of the Country* (1913), *Twilight Sleep* (1927), *Hudson River Bracketed* (1929), and *The Gods Arrive* (1932). Her most enduring novel was *Ethan Frome* (1911), which explores the grim and often anguished nature of New England farm life. *The Age of Innocence* (1920), which won a Pulitzer Prize, is considered her finest work.

She was divorced from Wharton in 1913. In 1923, on her last visit to the United States, she became the first woman to receive an honorary doctorate from Yale University. In all, she published more than 50 books, including fiction, poetry, travel books, and literary criticism. She died on Aug. 11, 1937, in St-Brice-sous-Forêt, France.

VIRGINIA WOOLF

(b. 1882–d. 1941)

English writer Virginia Woolf is best known as a novelist. However, she also was a noteworthy essayist and short-story writer.

Virginia Woolf was born Virginia Stephen in London on Jan. 25, 1882, and was educated by her father, Sir Leslie Stephen. After his death she set up housekeeping in Gordon Square in the district of Bloomsbury in London. Beginning in about 1907 her home was frequently visited by the young intellectuals who later became known as the Bloomsbury group. Among the group's members were economist John Maynard Keynes, biographer Lytton Strachey, novelist E.M. Forster, and political writer Leonard Woolf, the latter of whom became her husband in 1912. The couple founded Hogarth Press as a publisher for her own and other authors' books.

Her first novels—*The Voyage Out* (1915) and *Night and Day* (1919)—were praised by the critics, but she was dissatisfied with them and began to experiment with

Portrait of author Virginia Woolf. New York World-Telegram & Sun Collection/Library of Congress, Washington, D.C. (neg. no. LC-USZ62-111438)

stream-of-consciousness writing. This is a narrative technique in which the reader lives within the mind of the characters and watches the story unfold. Her first such work was *Jacob's Room* (1922), followed by *Mrs. Dalloway* (1925), *To the Lighthouse* (1927), and *The Waves* (1931). *Between the Acts* (1941) was her last novel.

Woolf was troubled by emotional problems for many years. During a period of disturbance she drowned herself in Sussex on March 28, 1941. In the decades after her death, her long essay, *A Room of One's Own* (1929), became a major text of the feminist movement. In it she describes the difficulties encountered by women writers in a society dominated by males.

Glossary

chivalry A code of conduct marked by honor, generosity, and courtesy.

colloquial Language, written or spoken, that is conversational and informal in tone.

Nonconformist One who does not conform to an established church, especially the Church of England.

notary An official clerk who draws up and certifies legal papers and documents.

oppression Unjust or cruel exercise of authority or power.

pamphleteer One who writes unbound materials that attack something or urge a cause.

pilgrimage A journey undertaken to a shrine or holy place.

propaganda The spreading of ideas, information, or rumor for the purpose of helping or injuring an institution, a cause, or a person.

protagonist The main character in a literary work.

royalties A payment to an author or composer for each copy of a work sold.

satire A literary work holding up human vices and follies to ridicule or scorn.

trilogy A series of three literary works that are closely related and develop a single theme.

For More Information

American Comparative Literature Association
University of South Carolina
Department of Languages, Literatures and Cultures
1620 College Street, Room 813A
Columbia, SC 29208
(803) 877-3021
The American Comparative Literature Association is a society for scholars whose work involves literatures and cultures from around the world. The organization offers news, publications, conferences, resource materials, and a directory of university comparative literature programs.

Association of Literary Scholars, Critics, and Writers
650 Beacon Street, Suite 510
Boston, MA 02215
(617) 358-1990
Web site: http://www.alscw.org
Founded in 1994, the Association of Literary Scholars, Critics, and Writers seeks to broaden the discourse around classic and contemporary literature. The organization offers resources for literary

study, promotes curricula for literature in schools, and highlights the exploration of links between literature and other art forms such as film, painting, or music.

National Book Foundation
90 Broad Street, Suite 604
New York, NY 10004
(212) 685-0261
Web site: http://www.nationalbook.org
Since 1950, the National Book Foundation has been the organization behind the National Book Awards (NBA), dedicated to recognizing and promoting the best in literary production in the United States. In addition to its NBA activities, the foundation also works to promote literacy and discussion of contemporary writing on high school and college school campuses and through reading clubs in cities across America.

PEN Canada
24 Ryerson Avenue, Suite 301
Toronto, ON M5T 2P3
Canada
(416) 703-8448
Web site: http://pencanada.ca

PEN Canada is dedicated to promoting and encouraging literature and the freedom of expression of the literary community in Canada. To that effort, the organization promotes the readership of popular writers, both international and Canadian, and discussion of their works and the contributions they have made to society at large. Its "Ideas in Dialogue" literary series hosts conversations with famous writers to reflect on their lives, works, and the importance of literary artistic freedom in society.

Penticton Writers and Publishers (PWAP)
4011 Finnerty Road
Penticton, BC V2A 8W2
Canada
(250) 492-0629
Web site: http://www.penwriters.com
Penticton Writers and Publishers is dedicated to promoting the writing and publishing industries in British Columbia. In addition to publishing anthologies of literature and hosting monthly writers groups, it plans events for teen readers in the area, including

the Raise a Reader youth literacy program.

Young Adult Library Services Association
50 East Huron Street
Chicago, IL 60611
(800) 545-2433 x4390
Web site: http://www.ala.org/yalsa
The goal of the Young Adult Library Services Association is to increase and strengthen library services for teenage readers. The group provides numerous grants and awards for young-adult literary research, conference attendance, and scholarship, and sponsors the annual Teen Read Week.

Web Sites

Due to the changing nature of Internet links, Rosen Educational Services has developed an online list of Web sites related to the subject of this book. This site is updated regularly. Please use this link to access the list:

http://www.rosenlinks.com/eafct/class

For Further Reading

Boon, Kevin A. *Ernest Heminway: The Sun Also Rises and Other Works*. New York, NY: Benchmark Books, 2008.

Brackett, Virginia. *Restless Genius: The Story of Virginia Woolf.* Greensboro, NC: Morgan Reynolds Publishing, 2004.

Dinsdale, Ann. *The Brontës at Haworth*. Islington, London, England: Francis Lincoln Publishers, 2013

Hensley, Laura. *The Story Behind F. Scott Fitzgerald's* The Great Gatsby. Chicago, IL: Heinemann-Raintree, 2007.

Houle, Michelle M. *Mark Twain: Banned, Challenged, and Censored.* Berkeley Heights, NJ: Enslow, 2008.

Meltzer, Milton. *Up Close: John Steinbeck*. New York, NY: Viking, 2008.

Murray, Albert, and John C. Callahan, eds. *Trading Twelves: The Selected Letters of Ralph Ellison and Albert Murray.* New York, NY: Vintage Books, 2001.

Reef, Catherine. *Jane Austen: A Life Revealed*. London, England: Clarion, 2011.

Sommers, Michael A. *J.D. Salinger*. New York, NY: Rosen Publishing, 2005.

Warren, Andrea. *Charles Dickens and the Street Children of London.* Boston, MA: Houghton Mifflin Harcourt, 2011.

Index

D

E

F

G

H